AZUSA STREET: THEY TOLD ME THEIR STORIES

The Youth and Children of Azusa Street
Tell Their Stories

Retold by Brother Tommy
A Life Transformed by the Azusa Story

Tom Welchel, Storyteller

Captured in Print by
Dr. J. Edward Morris and Cindy McCowan

AZUSA STREET:
THEY TOLD ME THEIR STORIES

The Youth and Children of Azusa Street
Tell Their Stories

Retold by Brother Tommy
A Life Transformed by the Azusa Story

Original Copyright © 2006,
Revised First Edition 2008, 2010
See the last page for details of copyright

Printed in the United States of America by
Dare 2 Dream Books 405-642-8257

Tom Welchel 405-410-9201

Publisher's Cataloging in Publication
Welchel, Tom
Azusa Street: They Told Me Their Stories
1. Christianity, 2. Inspirational, 3. Revival,
4. Historical
ISBN 0-9779688-0-4

DEDICATED
TO THE YOUTH OF THIS WORLD

The Azusa Street Experience was as much about what God was doing through teenagers and young people as it was about leaders such as William Seymour and Frank Bartleman.

The stories contained in this book are about young people performing miracles, exercising God's gifts, and witnessing about God's power. These are stories about young people being a vital part of one of the greatest outpourings of God's Presence in history.

If you are a teenager or young person, these stories are meant to inspire and encourage you. God can—and wants—to use you _now_, not sometime in the future when you "grow up." This book introduces you to many great Christians from the glorious Azusa Street meetings who went on to proclaim the message of God, and be used of Him in mighty ways. Some even were instrumental in helping start great religious movements such as the Assemblies of God. But, first they were touched and used by God when they were as young as twelve and thirteen years old.

Without question, God is orchestrating yet another great outpouring of His Shekinah Presence on this earth. The signs of His impending visitation are everywhere as even now revivals explode across the world.

Those of us dedicated to bringing these stories to the world are convinced that one of the main reasons that God ordained this book to be published at this time is to inspire our youth! Forty years after a prophecy that these words would be published, God brought together those He wanted to use to make it happen. Each and every one on this team believe that God wants young people to know that He can use them in a mighty way just as He did a century ago with the young men and women you will meet in the following pages.

That which was from the beginning, which we have heard, which we have seen with our eyes, which we have looked at and our hands have touched— this we proclaim.
I John 1:1 (KJV)

Table of Contents

312 Azusa Street

Foreword by Billye Brim

Charles Parham's granddaughter told me a few years ago about an amazing prophecy given through her grandfather. He prophesied that in about 100 years there would be another great outpouring of the Spirit of God to surpass what happened in Acts 2, Topeka, and Azusa. As you will read in this book, William Seymour also gave such a prophecy.

I had already seen this in Scripture. The former rain outpouring was Acts Two. The latter rain outpouring was the Azusa Revival 1906-1910. And the former and latter rain together, prophesied in Joel 2:23 and James 5:7, will precede the coming of the Lord.

This book, published 100 years after the Azusa outpouring, is filled with thrilling eye-witness accounts of the manifestation of the Glory of God and the resulting miracles that drew people from all over the world to the little warehouse in Los Angeles. I believe that this book is published at exactly the right time. I read it aloud in meetings, and the result is a manifestation of God's Presence and an extreme hunger for these things in the people of God. I read it aloud on my radio program, and our phones light up after each broadcast.

There are elements to an outpouring of God. There is a God part. And there is our part. On our part, one of those elements is prayer. This book will stir you up. It will stir up your congregation. It stirs us to believe, to pray, to expect, and to prepare our own lives—and, I believe, to the love and unity manifested in the congregation at Azusa.

Billye Brim

A BOOK OF MANY AUTHORS
Oral Traditions Captured in Print

The first authors of this book are the Saints of Azusa Street who relived the stories of Azusa over and over again. They captured the attention of a young man affectionately called Brother Tommy. He would not only cherish their stories but would hide them in his heart until God was ready to have them memorialized in print.

The second author of this book is Tom Welchel, or Brother Tommy. He spent hours upon hours listening to these dear Saints for several years, allowing these stories to be indelibly engraved in his mind. For forty years he waited for the right moment that God had ordained for him to share his stories with an writer/editor who would capture the essence of the stories in written form.

The third authors are Dr. J. Edward Morris and Cindy McCowan, who took this oral tradition, and staying true to the accounts recalled by Tom, crafted the stories into an organized record of events of Azusa. The stories and book are told through Tom's eyes. The personal references refer to Tom. Whenever a first person personal pronoun is used, it is referencing Tom.

The most important author is God, who ordained forty years ago that this oral tradition would become available to the world in print. God, in His magnificent power, has kept Tom's mind clear and precise, preserving these stories in minute detail.

A work concerning "Oral Traditions"

It is not unusual to find errors in oral traditions. Remember these stories were passed on to Brother Tommy over 40 years ago. We have made some corrections in this book and have researched questions folks have sent to us, and most of the time we have found Tommy's version to be correct.

If you feel you have information that will help us preserve these stories in their most accurate form, please contact the publisher at **dare2dreambooks@yahoo.com**, and we will diligently research your concerns and make any corrections necessary.

ACKNOWLEDGEMENTS

A Labor of Love

A special thank you goes to members of Faith Family Church in El Reno, Oklahoma, for their dedication to making this book become a reality. For several weeks, members met on Monday and Friday nights to listen to Tom tell the Azusa Street stories. Others would assist in transcribing the tapes from the weekly sessions. Pastors Paul and Samantha Roach gave invaluable support by opening their home each Monday and Friday night for the recording sessions. This was truly a labor of love as the excitement grew each week. Everyone involved understood how important it was to get a written record of these stories while Tom was able to recall them with clarity and detail. I want to especially thank Mary McMahan, Jennifer Williams, Bob Reese, Nicholas Karis, and Paul and Samantha Roach—the listening group who meet on a weekly basis.

A big "thank you" goes to those who transcribed the tapes. This group includes Samantha Roach, Gina Casey, Jana Ford, Lisa Cosentino, and Cindy McCowan.

Another group to which we deeply are indebted is the group of editors that assisted in making sure that the message is as error free as humanly possible. These editors include Lisa Consentino, Natalie Roach, Bob and Traci Clegg, Charles and Trelita Mickle, Gary and Jana Ford, Dr. Morris, Cindy McCowan, Mikkah Mickle, Mary McMahan, Jennifer Williams, Bob Reese, Nicholas Karis, and Paul and Samantha Roach.

PREFACE

Azusa Remembered

Azusa Street has been the topic of a multitude of books. Writers have attempted to tell the Azusa story from a historical perspective, a doctrinal perspective, and a personal perspective from those who had experienced the awesome outpouring of God's Spirit. What is unique about this book is that it is a compilation of stories about those who were there but were mostly mere children or young people.

These stories are fresh and revealing and are told from the eyes of youth as recalled up to sixty years later. The Saints recalled these stories over and over again in the mid-sixties to a young man called Brother Tommy. While these stories were being retold, the sixtieth anniversary of the Azusa Street Revival was being celebrated.

From a three-year-old child sleeping under the pews during the revival to other amazing, first-hand memories, Brother Tommy recounts the stories of Azusa Saints who had settled together at the Old Pisgah Home. This home had become a mission post that ministered to those who were less fortunate and in need of some sincere Christian ministering.

A Word Concerning
The Shekinah Glory

Throughout this book, you will read about the Shekinah Glory that fell on the Azusa Street Revival. Although the word "Shekinah" is not found in the Bible, the Jewish rabbis used this non-biblical term, which they derived from a Hebrew word that literally means "He caused to dwell", to signify that this dwelling was a divine visitation of the Presence of God on the earth.

The Shekinah Glory defines the mist or cloud that is present when God is physically present. In Exodus 24:16-17, we are told, "The glory of the Lord settled on Mount Sinai. For six days, the cloud covered the mountain and on the seventh day the Lord called to Moses from within the cloud. To the Israelites, the glory of the Lord looked like a consuming fire on top of the mountain."

The term "Shekinah Glory" is accurately and appropriately used to describe what happened at Azusa Street from 1906-1910.

DIVINE APPOINTMENTS

Foreword by the Editor

I made it a point to arrive early. I had no idea where I was going, and I had an important appointment with potential authors. As I drove into the Faith Family Church parking lot in El Reno, Oklahoma, 45 minutes prior to my appointment, Pastor Samantha Roach, who was about to leave, greeted me. Remember, I was 45 minutes early and just seconds before she was to leave the church, I "just happened" to run into the very person I was to meet with. She had forgotten about our appointment, and if I had not arrived exactly when I did, she would have been gone for the afternoon. Samantha apologized that she had double-booked her time and suggested we meet for lunch in an hour at a restaurant in Yukon.

Since there was another person in the parking lot of the church, and having time to kill, I greeted a man who introduced himself as Tom. We exchanged a few friendly words and then spent the next several minutes talking about the .357 magnum he had holstered on his side. Within minutes, I had met both the pastor and the man who, by divine appointment, "just happened" to be in the parking lot at that exact moment.

As I left the church parking lot, I could see Tom walk over to talk with his pastor. Little did I know that their brief meeting would turn out to be the fulfillment of a 40 year old prophecy.

Divine appointments! Forty years ago? Let me explain.

Four weeks earlier, I was driving up and down the streets of Oklahoma City calling on pastors and introducing our publishing ministry. I was having little to no success. Even though it was Wednesday, I could not find a pastor in his study anywhere. I called on Baptist Churches, Churches of God, Assemblies of God, and Nazarene Churches. Each time, the results were the same: Nobody was in. After about 90 minutes of this frustrating process, I had a clear message from God. I was told to go back to my office and call pastors in my hometown and in the neighboring town. With a huge sigh of resignation, I got on Interstate 40 and headed for Mustang.

I went right to my office, opened the phone book to the church listings and began to call. My very first call was to Faith Family Church. Pastor Paul Roach answered, and when I told him I was looking for pastors with a desire to publish, he asked me to hold while he got his wife, Samantha, on the phone. In response to my introduction, I discovered that they were interested in publishing and that they had been in the process of trying to find a publisher. We set a time to meet four weeks into the future, and I hung up certain that this truly was a

2

divine appointment—I just didn't know the magnitude of God's plan.

Four weeks later, I found myself at a restaurant with Paul and Samantha Roach and the man I had met in the parking lot—remember Tom, the man with the .357 magnum. My assumption was that Tom must have been the other appointment, and Samantha wisely combined the two meetings. My assumption was wrong. An hour earlier, God continued His intervention. Samantha had invited Tom to join us because she believed that he was a vital part of why we were meeting.

After brief introductions and a brief overview of my publishing company, Samantha explained why Tom had been invited to join us. Tom also had a message that needed to put into print.

Tom began to tell his story. It took me a few seconds to sort out what was happening. I discovered during the conversation that he was a private investigator—hence the cannon on his hip. I wasn't sure what his story was, but I was a captive audience—a man with a .357 magnum has my undivided attention. As Tom began to tell his story, I forgot about the gun. I knew immediately that his story—or stories—had to be told.

Now remember, my agenda was to meet with Paul and Samantha and set up the process to publish their books. But, on this day it wasn't about my agenda! It wasn't about Paul and Samantha's books. It was about a divine appointment between Tom, Paul and Samantha, myself, and God that had been written into God's day-timer forty years prior.

Through an amazing work of grace, back in 1960, Tom found himself at the feet of several "Azusa Street Saints" listening intently to their stories about this great Movement of God. Here's Tom's story in his own words about an amazing prophecy:

The woman that prophesied to me was Jean Darnall. She is the woman who took over for Aimee Semple-McPherson when she died in 1944. At Pisgah, they had this publication called the *Herald of Hope,* and there was quite a large mailing list of about a quarter of a million names or more.

If Jean was going to appear in some town, she would call Brother Smith and he would call me into his office and let me know what Jean needed. Then I would go and get that city's mailing list and some surrounding towns and with the envelopes Jean would send, I would print addresses for her.

It just so happens that one time there was going to be an international convention of the Full Gospel Businessmen's Fellowship in 1966, which was the 60th anniversary of Azusa, and it was to be held at Angelus Temple. Demos Shakarian, the founder of the Full Gospel Businessmen's Fellowship, had come to Brother Smith, who was a member of the board of Pisgah. He said that he wanted to get the Azusa Street Saints to come down to the convention and tell their stories. Well, they only had time for about three of them.

Jean Darnall was coming to Pisgah to get some envelopes I had finished, and stopped by to see some of the ladies who were to tell their stories. During conversations, several of the ladies told Jean, "If you ever want to get the whole story, go talk to Brother Tommy over there at the *Herald of Hope,* because he knows every one of the Saints' stories and can tell 'um better and more accurately than we can." That's exactly where Pastor Darnall headed next.

Jean Darnall came to the *Herald of Hope* office and when she saw me, she just looked at me and said, "Brother Tommy, come over here, I have a word from the Lord for you. The Lord is showing me that all these stories that the Azusa Street Saints have been telling you, and you have been learning and memorizing, will some day will be put into a book."

I thanked her for her kind words, thought about what she had said, and then hid her words in my heart. I'm not one that goes and starts trying to make God's prophecies come to pass. If it's prophesied to me, I just

5

never forget 'em; I never do forget, but I let God take care of it. He will work the timing out. What is it now, 40 years later? He's working it out for the 100-year anniversary.

I remember a Christian song that was popular many years ago. The lyrics said, "God has something to say to you, God has something to say. Listen, listen, pay close attention, God has something to say." I don't think there is a better application for these lyrics than the message in this book. God has waited 40 years to have these stories told. That is significant. Noah was on the Ark for 40 days. The Children of Israel wandered 40 years in the desert. Saul, David, and Solomon each ruled 40 years each. Jesus was tempted for 40 days. And now God waits 40 years to keep this divine appointment. I think that if God had a specific time in mind to publish this message, there must be a divine reason. The stories that are told in this book are of particular relevance for today's generation of Saints, and I believe are even the seeds of a new outpouring of God's Spirit. William Seymour and others prophesied during the days of Azusa that there would be another great revival and outpouring of the Shekinah Glory around the turn of the next century.

INTRODUCING BROTHER TOMMY

As many of the Azusa Street Saints were migrating to Pisgah, being drawn there to join other Saints for fellowship and divine purpose, Tom Welchel was headed to Pisgah from Chickasha, Oklahoma. God had a divine appointment with Tom and these dear Saints. Just as Jesus told His disciples that He needed to go to Samaria because God had a divine appointment set with the woman at the well, Tom would keep two God-ordained appointments: his Venice Beach appointment and his Pisgah appointment. The first appointment had to do with his salvation and the second appointment had to do with God's plans for Tom—including a plan that would span four decades before it was fulfilled.

At the age of 17, Tom thought he was running from the law as he headed for California. What he didn't know is that God had prepared for him a homecoming of the prodigal son and that he was running right into the open arms of God Himself.

Recalling his childhood, Tom noted,

> Mama took me to all the great revivals—tent revivals. I'm talking about Brannum, Cole, Allen, and Roberts. From a little bitty kid on up, Mama would take me to

'em. I didn't know what was going on—she just wanted to punish me as far as I was concerned.

When I saw Brannum in 1954, I was only 11 years old. I saw that halo thing on top of his head when he was in Houston. I was glad I was sitting way in the back—scared the tullies out of me. That was one man I didn't want to get close to.

So, I knew about the Gospel, but I didn't want it at that time. I was fourteen when I stopped going to revivals—almost fifty years ago. By the time I was fourteen, I was no longer afraid of Mama. In the past, if I got mean, she would say, "Alright, I'll talk to your Daddy." Well I didn't want Daddy to talk to me because he had a razor strap that would cut the blood right out of me and he would use it.

But my daddy went to the state prison in McAllister when I was 14—the revenuers caught him selling corn liquor.

By the time Tom was seventeen, he had been living on the streets for fourteen months and was a criminal wanted by the police. Society was pretty much fed up with his lawlessness and was ready to lock him up and if possible, throw away the key. According to Tom, the police wanted him and were looking for him big time. Here are Tom's own words:

An old friend of mine, Glen, came by and said, "Tommy, the police know who's been breaking in all those houses. They told me they have my finger prints." So I says, "I guess I'm going back to prison."

"The cops say, 'No! We want Welchel! We're gonna get him off the streets and the rest of you'll split up.' In fact, they have a warrant for your arrest and they are gonna come by and get you.'"

But God had a different plan. God would use Tom's choice to run from the law as a life-changing decision. Tom could escape the reach of the law from Chickasha, Oklahoma, by running to California, but he couldn't escape the reach of God's love.

Tom tells the story like this:

A guy named Teddy and his grandma, who were con artists, wanted me to go to California with them. Things were rough in Oklahoma. More than once, Teddy got his teeth knocked out, his nose broken, and his eyes blackened cuz he would smart off.

They were from Venice Beach and they wanted to go back, and they invited me to go with 'em cuz I had a reputation as a good thief—I could be sitting there talking to you and leave with the stuff from your pockets in mine.

I didn't really want to go to California and leave Oklahoma, but Glen reminded me that it was either go to California or go to jail. So I went to Grandma and Teddy and asked if the offer was still open to me.

They said "Yeah." I told them okay, but that I had two big boxes of loot that we needed to go and get early in the morning—stuff I'd stolen. So the next morning we got my stuff and I got to runnin' from the authorities to keep from going to prison.

When we got to Venice Beach, Teddy and I got into a fight over a girl. I didn't get the girl, but I whipped Teddy. Grandma said, "Look, I don't care. I like you Tommy, but you can't stay here with you and Teddy fighting like this. You hurt him pretty bad!" So I got kicked out—lost my place to stay—and the girl.

The stage was set for God's loving intervention. God used the fact that Grandma and Teddy were from Venice Beach in a powerful way. Tom was back on the streets but in an unfamiliar world. His situation was ripe for him to continue his lawless ways just to survive. But remember, Tom wasn't alone. Grandma may have turned her back on Tom, but God had not abandoned him. Those childhood years of sitting under the ministries of the great revivalists of that time planted seeds that were soon to be harvested. Mama's faithfulness in bringing up her child in the atmosphere of God's Word would not go unrewarded. Tom was about to meet God like he had never experienced Him in the past. Tom continues his story:

I'm down on Venice Beach, not knowin' what to do. It was probably four or five in the evening. I'm sitting there thinking, "What am I gonna do?" Uncle Ed lived in California but he was up there in Bakersfield and I didn't know which way Bakersfield was.

Then I saw these two old ladies walkin' down there, and I was sure they were lookin' for someone to witness to. Well, I'm sitting there with this long face, feeling sorry for myself, not knowin' where to go or what to do. I was really mad cuz the girl could have at least been nice, and now I am all alone feelin' sorry for myself.

These two ladies came over and sat down, one on each side of me, and started talking to me. One of the ladies was the landlord at the apartment where Grandma and Teddy lived. The other lady, kinda small and dainty, was called Sister Goldie.

Sister Goldie did most of the talking while the Landlord sat there and held my hand. That felt good—she reminded me of both of my grandmas. They were talking about the Lord, and Sister Goldie asked if I knew anything about Him. I said, "Yeah, my grandparents were devout Christians and would tell me and my mother about the Lord."

When they asked me if I wanted to pray the sinner's prayer, I decided why not, what have I got to lose? I thought, "Man, you're here; you don't know anybody. What else are you gonna do?" At first, I really wasn't serious but rather kinda in my "con" mode. But as soon as I said the prayer, to my astonishment, I felt something warm come all over me, and I began to cry. I looked at them and again to my surprise, I told them that I was now a Christian.

Somehow these two women broke through a wall that had been built up for years. Preaching to me never worked. I'd rebel and you didn't want to get me mad. I was libel to hurt you. I said the prayer for these ladies because I was hoping these women would do something for me. It was time to eat and I was hungry.

Even though I began the prayer insincerely, God heard it, and it was like I just had a heater go off in me. The love and kindness of these dear women touched me deeply. That day, that prayer changed me completely.

Tom's divine appointment had been kept. Tom took a 1500-mile journey that brought him to two sweet ladies whose love ushered Tom into his new life with Christ. The power of the Gospel caught Tom at a very vulnerable time. He had hit bottom with no place to go and all of the sudden he was touched by love. Two grandmotherly-type women who reminded Tom of his grandmothers—perhaps the only two people who had ever been kind to Tom—touched his soul. So the plan of God unfolded as Tom was led from Chickasha, Oklahoma to Venice Beach, California. But that was just the beginning of God's awesome plan.

After Tom told the ladies of his predicament, they brought him back to the landlord's apartment where he spent the night. The next morning, Sister Goldie returned to take Tom to a place called Pisgah—Tom's ultimate destination!

Upon arrival at the Pisgah community, Sister Goldie introduced Tom to many of her friends—Azusa Saints who had moved to Pisgah. In 1960, Tom would meet many whose lives were touched and changed by Azusa. These were the children and youth of the Azusa Street Revival, now retired or near retirement. For six years, Tom would literally sit at the feet of these Saints and listen over and over again to their stories about the Azusa Street Revival and its impact on their lives.

Early leaders of the Azusa Street Mission, 1907
William J. Seymour front, second from right

THE PISGAH CONNECTION

In July of 1894, Dr. Yoakum was critically injured while on his way to organize a Class Leader's Association for his Methodist Church. He was struck by a piece of metal extending from a buggy operated by a drunken man. The piece of metal pierced his back, broke several ribs, and caused internal hemorrhaging. The wounds were so severe, a medical examination of his injuries showed that the injuries should have been fatal.

Due to the extent of his injuries and the infection that lasted for several months, Dr. Yoakum moved to Los Angeles hoping that the milder climate would give him relief from his suffering. The climate helped, but his relief came in the form of a miraculous healing from the ministry of W. C. Stevens. Dr. Yoakum, almost in desperation, visited a Christian Alliance Church on Figueroa Street in Highland Park. There, Pastor Stevens prayed for him, and he was instantly healed.

That was in February of 1895. By that summer, he had moved to Highland Park and opened up his mission in fulfillment of visions he had directing him to create a mission for the needy. Giving up his medical practice, he vowed to spend the remainder of his life serving the chronically ill, poor and destitute, and social outcasts.

15

During the Azusa Street Revival gatherings in Los Angeles in 1906 and 1907, Yoakum hosted many followers at the Mission site in Highland Park. The Mission was named Pisgah Home after the Mountain where Moses stood to view the Promised Land. Now you can understand the Azusa connection.

Dr. Yoakum was extremely important to the continued effects of Azusa Street in a very practical way. He often gave his workers pockets full of nickels, then told them to go down to the skid row area of Los Angeles and provide passage by way of a streetcar to Avenue 60 (the fare to ride was five cents). From Avenue 60, they walked one block to Pisgah where they were allowed to stay and become part of the community. It wasn't long before Pisgah became a large community. Again, it is important to point out that the ministry to skid row started by Dr. Yoakum was still ongoing when Brother Tommy arrived in the Sixties.

After the death of Dr. Yoakum in 1920, Christ Faith Mission, Inc. purchased Pisgah Home under the direction of Arglee Green. Sister Green and her sister restored Pisgah Home and renamed it "Echo Home."

Aimee Semple-McPherson conducted services at the Arroyo Seco River during the 1920's to tens of thousands of worshipers who later retreated to the Mission site for massive barbecues and meetings.

In 1950, Reverend Harold James Smith came to manage the mission operations with a vision for revival. Reverend Smith re-named the site, "Old Pisgah Home," restoring its historic name. He also began a publication of a salvation and healing newsletter called the *Herald of Hope.*

By the time Reverend Smith took over, many Azusa Street Saints had come and settled at Pisgah. A variety of reasons drew them there such as fellowship and the opportunity to minister to those who gathered at Pisgah.

By the time Brother Tommy arrived in 1960, Pisgah had become home for many of the Saints of Azusa who were mere children and young people back in the 1906 revival at 312 Azusa Street.

November 17, 2006

Dear Friends,

We are privileged to recommend Brother Tommy Welchel to you. He endeared himself to many Azusa Street Saints during his stay at Pisgah in 1960-1966 and had a marvelous bond with them—always loving to listen to their stories of days gone by. Our father, known to all as Brother H. J. Smith, was pastor at that same time that Tommy was at Pisgah and we resided on the grounds with our family. Indeed our father's pastoral ministry was truly that of a dedicated life for others including being Tommy's Pastor while he resided at Pisgah.

Vivian (Smith) Detiege
and Viola (Smith) Hoover

(Vivian and Viola are the daughters of the Harold Smith mentioned throughout the book.)

Brother Tommy in 1962, age 19
Wearing the clothes that Sister Goldie purchased for him (pg. 112)

Feburary 4, 1991

Dear Pisgah Alumni:

Nova Seals and I have been in touch and thought it would be great for all of us to get together for a reunion of all who attended Pisgah in Highland Park.... I would appreciate your input soon so we can get the plans started.

Ruth (Milke)Rinker

818-353-5434

INTRODUCTION TO
THEY TOLD ME THEIR STORIES

When I got to Pisgah, I soon realized that many of the people there had been a part of the great Azusa Revival. As I heard people talk about Azusa Street, I said to myself, "Wait a minute, Momma talked about this Azusa Street thing. Some of the preachers that Momma would take me to hear would talk about Azusa Street." Brother Smith, the overseer of Pisgah, told me more about the revival and also told me who at Pisgah had experienced Azusa.

I was so shy back then. I was afraid to go talk to these Saints until one of the Saints, Brother Cantrell, prayed that I be given the gift of "holy boldness." After he performed that miracle in my life, I went down on skid row and witnessed to the men and women there about Jesus. No longer shy, I started going to these different Saints at Pisgah and asking to hear their stories.

I was privileged as a teenager—I wasn't but 17—when I first started sitting and listening to these old Azusa Street Saints. I spent several years getting to know quite a few of these dear Saints of God.

I heard the stories of the Azusa Street Saints over and over, every month for years until they died or until I left. I went to their apartments or wherever they were.

19

Most of them lived on the grounds of Pisgah, but a few lived elsewhere. It didn't make any difference; wherever they were, I would walk to them. Once in their homes, to show respect, I'd sit down at their feet. Of course, I had told them that I liked chocolate chip cookies and milk. So when I'd go to hear their stories, they had cookies and milk for me. I never grew tired of sitting with each person—sometimes up to a few hours—so I could hear these great Saints share their memories of the incredible move of God and His use of these willing and faithful teens at Azusa Street. I've got the stories right here in my head where they have been for over forty years.

William Seymour and his wife Jenny Moore

AZUSA FROM UNDER THE PEW

Meet Sister Darnall

As they turned the corner, the little three-year-old could see the dingy white warehouse that people crowded into 24 hours a day. Although she was just over three years old, the journey was a daily affair and with the evening dampness in the air, she couldn't wait to get inside the Azusa Street meeting place. Now a daily tradition, she would take in all the excitement that filled the room, marveling and wondering about all that was happening around her. Although the child didn't understand why people were shouting and crying, nor the miracles that were taking place, she liked the atmosphere. But, what she liked most was that in a few minutes after entering the room, Mom would find her seat and she would be able to crawl under the pew, get comfortable, and take a nap.

This toddler had also become comfortable with the thick mist that filled the room. Being in a playful mood when she woke up from her nap, she would try to gather the mist into her arms. She loved the cloud that filled the Azusa Street Warehouse for almost three and one-half years during what is now historically called the Azusa Street Revival. It would be a few years before she was old enough to understand that she was trying to capture the Shekinah Glory of God.

21

As a mere child, she literally breathed the Shekinah Glory into her young, developing lungs. She experienced Azusa through the eyes and mind of a young toddler. Although her mind could not comprehend all that was going on around her, she knew she was in a very special place among some very special people at a very special time.

As she grew older, she would learn of the miracles and Presence of God in the form of the Shekinah Glory— so thick during those meetings—where she found comfort under the pew. She would be able to tie together the experiences recalled by family and friends with the experiences her heart captured but her mind was unable to comprehend at that tender age.

This story was told by Jean Darnall, who followed in the steps of Aimee Semple-McPherson. Without question this story had a profound effect on her life and ministry. When I met her, she was in her early forties, and I was a somewhat permanent fixture at Pisgah. A dark haired woman, with a few streaks of gray accenting her attractiveness, Sister Darnall was quiet and soft-spoken, standing about five feet and four inches. Anyone that met her fell in love with her sweet, gentle nature.

I share her story of this child because it illustrates how Azusa impacted even the youngest of children. But also to introduce Jean Darnall (Darnell). Jean played an important role in my life for she also was the person who told me something forty years ago that was finding fulfillment on the one-hundredth anniversary of the Azusa Street Revival.

The impact of the story of the three-year-old would be life-long for Sister Darnall. Her exposure to God and His mighty works would come throughout her youth as her mother took her to meetings such as those at the mission on Eighth and Maple led by Frank Bartleman. Although the great Shekinah Glory was unique to Azusa, and the story of the child happened some fifteen years prior to her birth, young Miss Darnall loved to hear the stories of Azusa and the time she spent at Eighth and Maple.

In 1944, she found herself to be one of the successors to the pulpit of the famed Aimee Semple-McPherson at Angelus Temple. I personally had attended many of her meetings at Angelus Temple and marveled at her anointing when she preached the Word of God.

This mighty preacher of God would often talk of the three-year-old's experience at Azusa and about the Shekinah Glory that she had fallen in love with and tried to capture. That experience was so profound that it would be a part of her very soul.

Although Pastor Jean was not as demonstrative as Aimee Semple-McPherson, she was in many ways a better preacher. Normally quiet and soft-spoken, when she began to preach or teach, an anointing would come upon her and you could feel God's power within her. I will never forget what it was like to have Pastor Jean pray for me and lay her hands on my head. Whenever she laid hands on me and prayed for me, I felt the Spirit of God through her touch and tender words.

Pastor Darnall had taken a special liking to some of the young people around Pisgah, including me. Whenever she came to Pisgah to speak, she always made it a point to come early to spend time with some of my friends and me. Because of her willingness to talk with us on a personal level, I had the privilege of knowing and spending time with Pastor Darnall on several occasions. Once, when I asked her why she chose to spend time with Mike and me, she said, "You two men are very young, but you know what you are doing and you know God!" Coming from her lips, I took that as a great compliment.

My relationship with Pastor Darnall was one that I cherish to this day. Her compassion and care were instrumental in helping me develop as a young Christian. Today, I have no doubt that God ordained our relationship. In fact, Pastor Darnall is indirectly responsible for this book being written forty years later.

In 1966, the Full Gospel Businessmen's Fellowship was having its international convention at Angelus Temple and was planning to celebrate the sixtieth anniversary of the Azusa Street Revival. Demos Shakerien, the founder of the Full Gospel Businessmen's Fellowship, had come to Pisgah to talk to Brother Smith, who oversaw the Pisgah ministry. Shakerien wanted to get some of the Azusa Saints who were living at Pisgah to come to Angelus Temple and tell their stories.

Jean Darnall, the pastor of Angelus Temple, came to Pisgah. While waiting for some envelopes to be addressed that she had ordered from *Herald of Hope*, she visited with some of the Azusa Saints about coming and telling their stories at the convention. One of the Saints Pastor Jean talked to was Lucille, her former secretary. She explained what Shakerien was wanting and Lucille told Pastor Darnall, "If you really want to know all the stories, all you need to do is to get Brother Tommy Welchel to go to the convention and tell the stories. He knows all the stories down pat." Then Sister Carney, who we will introduce in the next chapter, said, "He knows them better than we do."

Jean Darnall left these Saints and came over to the *Herald of Hope* where I worked to pick up some envelopes I was addressing for her. As she drove over, she pondered what she had been told about me and my knowledge of the stories about Azusa, and during a time of prayer, the Lord spoke to her concerning my future. I came out to put the addressed envelopes in her car, and while she was getting out of the car to open the trunk, she called for me. Her words were simple but stunning. "Brother Tommy, come over here; I have a word from the Lord for you. The Lord is showing me that all these stories that the Azusa Street Saints have been telling you, and you have been learning and memorizing will someday be put into a book."

I thanked her for the word from God, but never intentionally tried to make it happen. I told a few of the

Saints and Brother Smith about Pastor Darnall's word from God, but other than that, I just kept her words in my heart. I want to be clear that I did not personally seek out anyone to write these stories. In fact, I was surprised when my pastors suggested that we make a record of these accounts. When we began to record the stories, I finally told one of my pastors about the prophesy from forty years ago. God is not slack in His promises. His revelation to Pastor Darnall now finds fulfillment according to His perfect timetable.

IN THE BEGINNING

Meet Sister Carney
Azusa Age: 17

The police officers were polite, yet firm. "Either shut it down or rent a place like a regular church or auditorium. You have gotten too big to continue to meet at this home."

This revival meeting began as a small gathering led by William Seymour in a home on Bonnie Brae Street. It now flowed out to the front yard, the neighbors' yards and onto the street as Brother Seymour preached from the porch of this small home in the Los Angeles area.

Seymour had been warned several times before and realized that he needed a much larger gathering place. The power of God was evident as the crowd grew larger and larger each passing day. He had been looking for a place to meet and had found an abandoned warehouse that at one time was used as a Methodist Church. The warehouse was perfect, and the only thing that was keeping Seymour from renting the building was money.

That night, the need to move was heavy on Seymour's heart. He prayed to God for direction and before the evening was over, he had received his answer.

God instructed him to get on a trolley car as soon as the service ended and to go to Pasadena.

True to God's leadership, Seymour didn't argue, but rather, headed for Pasadena where it was illegal for blacks like Brother Seymour, to be after dark. He rode the trolley until God instructed him to get off, and then followed as God directed him to an apartment nearby.

Sister Carney, just a teenager but married, had arrived in Pasadena earlier that day. She was to meet with several of her friends who had been members of the First Baptist Church until they had received the Baptism of the Holy Spirit. Somehow that didn't fit Baptist doctrine. This evening they were coming together to pray for revival.

Meeting together for months now in the apartment of one of the members of the group, this particular evening these ladies continued in fervent prayer for several hours. They were certain that God was about to do something big in the Los Angeles area.

Just after 10:00 p.m., God brought together two elements of a force that, when joined together, would usher in one of the greatest manifestations of God ever experienced by man since the birth of Christ.

Seymour walked up to the apartment that God had led him to and knocked on the door. Sister Carney remembers the time to be about 10:30 p.m. The ladies went to the door together and when they opened the door, found a black man, blind in one eye, standing before them. For many people in that day and in that area, a black man showing up at their door late at night would have been a sign to slam the door and call the police. But that night, God was in charge. The owner of the apartment, with some apprehension, asked, "Can I help you?" The answer to this simple, and somewhat fretful question would startle and astonish those gathered for prayer. After several months of fervent prayer, God responded in an unusual manner.

Seymour replied, "You're praying for revival, right?" When the ladies responded with a unanimous "yes," Seymour made a bold statement: "I'm the man God has sent to preach that revival."

Without hesitation, the ladies invited Seymour in. After some exciting chatter, he preached to them and took up an offering that was more than enough to rent the Azusa Street Warehouse.

This story is told to introduce Sister Carney. The prayer meeting that evening and those present at the meeting were not coincidental. God had been preparing many for the miracle of Azusa. Without this ordained meeting, Azusa may have never happened and the meeting would have never taken place had it not been for the work of Sister Carney.

Her story begins two years prior to Azusa. In 1904, Brother Lankford, whose story you will read later, returned from attending Bible school in Topeka, Kansas, which was under the leadership of Charles Parham. Coming back to Pisgah, Lankford met with Dr. Yoakum, the founder of Pisgah, and introduced him to the infilling of the Holy Spirit with the evidence of speaking in other tongues. Dr. Yoakum immediately embraced this teaching and began to share this experience with all that came to his meetings. While attending services at Pisgah, at the young age of fifteen, and already married, Sister Carney responded to Dr. Yoakum's teaching and was one of the first to receive the Baptism of the Holy Spirit.

In 1904, her love for the Lord and her desire to introduce others to the exciting experience of being filled with the Holy Spirit led her to Pasadena. There she witnessed to several of her friends who were members of the First Baptist Church. By 1906, these ladies had been asked to leave the Baptist Church because of their beliefs. Unknown to them, God was setting the stage for a miraculous work of the Holy Spirit.

When I met Sister Carney in the early sixties, she was in her mid seventies, standing about five feet, nine inches tall with a slender build of about 130 pounds. She was a typical little old granny, with a glory bun sitting on top of her gray hair. She walked slowly with short steps always wearing a pleasant smile. She had an older face with a little pointed chin and when she smiled her lips kind of sunk in. She still wore those flowery dresses ladies wore at the turn of the century. And yes, she wore granny boots—those little boots with little hooks and eyes.

About every third Monday night, I would walk to Sister Carney's apartment. As I approached her home, I would smell the enticing aroma of fresh baked chocolate chip cookies waiting for me. I had the privilege once a month of sitting at Sister Carney's feet on a small throw rug in front of her wooden rocker. While eating cookies and drinking a cold glass of milk, I listened to her tell her Azusa stories like the one that begins this chapter.

Appreciated by everyone because she could tell the stories of Azusa in detail better than anyone, Sister Carney was also one of my favorite storytellers. Although she normally had a little high-pitched voice, when she told her stories, her voice was soothing, yet filled with excitement.

The story we began with concerning the start of Azusa didn't end there. In the beginning, Sister Carney, then 17 years old, was there. In fact, Mrs. Carney was there from raising the rent for the building, to the first day they entered to clean the building, until they padlocked the door.

Sister Carney told of those first days at Azusa Street with an excitement that had stayed with her for over sixty years. Even with the money Seymour raised for the rent from Sister Carney and her friends, the old, dingy white warehouse still needed a lot of physical labor to get it ready for use.

Sister Carney and her friends from the apartment joined the group from Bonnie Brae to prepare the dirty, cluttered building to serve as a worship center. They removed all sorts of junk that had accumulated through the years. The warehouse had even been used as a barn,

31

housing all sorts of animals, and with the animals came mounds of animal waste.

Sister Carney recalls that Brother Seymour assigned each of the volunteers an area to clean. With a warm smile, she told how grateful she was for the task of cleaning up the area that housed the small goats with their small droppings rather than cleaning up after the horses and cattle.

After cleaning out the warehouse, the volunteers gathered and set up wooden fruit crates they had found thrown away behind the nearby grocery store. They placed 2 by 12 planks, twelve feet long to serve as benches throughout the meeting room. With only meager funds and their ingenuity, these volunteers labored side by side until the meeting place was ready to be used however God desired to use it—thankful that God had provided them a place large enough to house the anticipated services.

During one of those Monday night meetings, I asked Sister Carney, "What miracle do you remember that happened through you?" She smiled and her lips kind of sunk in as the excitement welled up inside her.

"It was the woman who caught her husband with another woman. She had gotten into a fight with her and the adulterous woman bit off her ear." Sister Carney was smiling but I laughed out loud. She gently chided me for laughing and said, "Brother Tommy, it's not funny to catch your husband with another woman and then for the two of them get to fighting and then the other woman bites the wife's ear off."

Here's the story as I recall. When the wife entered the meeting room, she was holding a bloody bandage to the side of her head. Sister Carney noticed she appeared to be in tremendous pain and went over to minister to her. While waiting for Seymour to come down and the meeting to begin, Sister Carney asked her what had happened, and the lady told her about the fight. She told her that she didn't have the ear with her, and Sister Carney reached over and kind of pulled the bandage off to see the wound that basically looked like a bloody, raw piece of meat. Without hesitation, she began to pray for the woman. After praying for her, the lady said that the pain was gone so Sister Carney looked at her wound again, and to her astonishment, right before her very eyes, a brand new ear began to grow out. Sister Carney sat there with her mouth open and simply exclaimed, "Oh my God!"

This wasn't the first miracle that Sister Carney witnessed, but it was the first one she witnessed as a result of God working through her own prayers. As she told me this story, she recalled it as if the miracle had just happened the night before.

I asked Sister Carney about other miracles she witnessed or participated in. With a smile and a twinkle in her eyes, she talked about the mighty works of God. According to Sister Carney, many people were there in wheelchairs and cots brought in from the hospitals around the area. Often, before Seymour would come downstairs or even when he was sitting with the box on his head, Sister Carney and others would go to the sick and crippled and pray for them, and they would get their healing. She and the others would go to those in wheelchairs, pull up the footrests, pray for them, and then watch them walk off, pushing their empty wheelchairs.

One of these wheelchair healings stayed with Sister Carney in a special way. One man had heavy braces on his legs and had not walked in years. She recalls that the wheelchair he was in had wheels made of wood. She prayed for him, and he was miraculously healed. His name was Brother Aubrey, and he was pastor of a big church in Los Angeles. I actually got to meet him because he would come to Pisgah to see his precious Sister Carney because she was the one who had prayed for him when he was healed at Azusa.

During one visit to Pisgah in the sixties, Brother Aubrey shared his version of the healing miracle. Sister Carney didn't say a word to him. She just walked up, pulled the footrests up, put his foot down, then got the other foot, lifted it up—remember his legs had very heavy braces on them—then laid it down. Next, she told him to get up and walk, but Aubrey told her he couldn't walk because of the heavy braces. Sister Carney responded by getting the people with him to take off his braces so he could walk. They did, and he did! He got up and walked.

I was amazed at the story and asked Sister Carney about how many miracles God had used her to personally perform. She told me that God blessed her by using her two to three times a day the three to four days she attended each week. That's six to eight miracles a week for over three and one-half years. Sister Carney explained that miracles abounded at Azusa. People with bones twisted were restored. You could hear bones popping and see arms and legs growing out.

Our talks turned from miracles performed by God through faithful saints attending the meetings to the difference in miracles when Brother Seymour was preaching. Sister Carney explained that when Brother Seymour would come down, there were even greater miracles. Seymour never had a set pattern; rather he would come down and put the box over his head and then later would take the box off when directed by God, get up and do what God told him to do.

Sometimes, he would go to a certain section of wheelchairs or to a certain section of cots—the cots were for people who had been carried in from the hospital. She explained that to her astonishment, Seymour would point at them and say, "Everyone on the cots or wheelchairs, you're healed in the Name of Jesus." Everyone on the cots or in wheelchairs would get up and walk around fully healed of whatever malady they suffered from

Some of the greatest miracles were when the flames were above the building. Bones that were cracked and broken were totally healed.

Our conversation would turn from the miracles performed by Seymour to Seymour personally. I wanted to know about this great man, and Sister Carney was a treasure chest of information. Her story began with the box on his head.

When Seymour came down to the meeting, he would sit down and put a box on his head. At first, it startled Sister Carney. Sometimes he would sit with the box over his head for ten minutes and sometimes it would be an hour or more. Although the practice seemed ridiculous, Sister Carney realized that he was obeying God, no matter how silly or ridiculous it appeared. That apparent act of humble obedience led to mighty power when he removed the box. This box and act of humility were critical to the power God displayed through Brother Seymour. When Brother Smith asked Sister Carney what caused the miracles and Azusa to stop, she replied, "It stopped when Brother Seymour stopped putting that box over his head. When he quit coming down and putting the box on his head, it started dying."

Seymour and Sister Carney became friends, and after Seymour married, Sister Carney would often join them for dinner. Even in a social setting she would feel the anointing on Seymour. She recalled that Seymour was very pleasant to be around. He was a humble man who always had a gleam in his eye, a smile on his face, and a deep, resonating voice.

There was no question about his anointing of God. She recalled that if you touched Seymour, a kind of electricity would shock you. The current was so strong that the first time she touched him during a meeting she almost passed out.

Of course, any discussion about Azusa turned to the Shekinah Glory. When I asked about her experience with the Presence of God's Spirit, Sister Carney's face would light up. She described it as being a part of heaven. To her, it was like breathing pure oxygen, and to her wonderment, it was always present.

When I asked her to describe the Shekinah Glory Fire reported by many, she told her story. She recalled the fire department coming because of a call that the building was on fire. When they arrived, they didn't smell any smoke or see any evidence of fire. She didn't run out with the firemen. She remembered that it was Seymour, Bosworth, Lake, Smith, and Sines that ran out.

Sister Carney did go out one time to see the flames for herself. Remember, the fire department had been called on several different occasions, as passers-by would report seeing flames leaping up from the roof of the building. Finally, Sister Carney asked John Lake why the fire department kept coming and looking for the fire. He explained that the fire was coming down from heaven into the building and fire was going up from the building and meeting the fire coming down. Fascinated, Sister Carney went out, walked about a half a block and saw the awesome sight for herself. To her, this divine connection of fire coming down from heaven and going up to heaven was just further evidence of God's mighty Presence in that place.

Sister Carney noted that although the Shekinah Glory was present all the time within the building, this divine connection wasn't an everyday occurrence. Whenever this connection was present, the power of God was even more intense within the meeting.

Sister Carney was a wealth of information. As we talked, she would mention some of the other young people she had associated with at Azusa. She was not the only young person running around being used of God to perform His miracles. She was kind of a team with C.W. Ward and Ralph Riggs, and she would invite them to go with her as new people arrived and see if they could minister to them. These young men were around 13 or 14 years old, partnering with Sister Carney, going through the crowd, wanting to be used by God to perform miracles and help people get healed. These were kids running around having a ball, praying over people and looking for people who needed healing. (These two young men would later become instrumental in helping to found The Assemblies of God Church, the largest Pentecostal Movement in the United States and the world.)

Sister Carney was also very close to John G. Lake, who had received the Baptism up in Zion, Illinois, and came to Azusa as a young man to see what was happening. He later became a great missionary and was used mightily in South Africa.

She also recounts her friendship with Brother Fox while he was at Azusa for about a year and one-half when he was around eighteen years old. Brother Fox later became a missionary in India. In fact, Fox came back to the States and Pisgah around 1963. He had retired from the mission field and settled at Pisgah, where the friendships with Sister Carney and other Azusa Saints were renewed.

Sister Carney is what I would call an Azusa legacy. She validates the mighty workings of God and the Presence of His Glory through the eyes of a young person in her late teens. Not only was she there as an eyewitness observer, she was also a vital participant in this awesome work of God. Her excitement and enthusiasm as she relived these stories with me each month allowed me to experience Azusa through her eyes. Truly, like John the Apostle*, she shared with me that which she had heard, she had touched with her hands, had seen with her own eyes, and experienced in her own heart from the beginning.

*1 John 1:1

Bonnie Brae House

A MODERN DAY ZACCHAEUS

Meet Brother Anderson

Azusa age: 15

The Azusa Street Warehouse filled quickly in anticipation of seeing and hearing Brother Seymour as he proclaimed the Word of God. The crowds had grown from a handful of faithful followers to hundreds now gathering several times a day to witness and experience the miracles of Azusa and the anointing of Brother Seymour.

Among those attending was a fifteen-year-old named Brother Anderson, who attended the Azusa Street Revival faithfully. He was one of first to receive the Baptism of the Holy Spirit at Azusa and be a part of this mighty work of God. Although he was just a few inches under six feet tall, when the crowd gathered, Brother Anderson often found it difficult to see what was happening throughout the building as miracles were being performed by many of his teenage friends.

The sight of Brother Anderson climbing on top of the benches was not uncommon. Like Zaccaeus of old, who climbed into a Sycamore tree to get a better view of Jesus, Anderson wanted a better vantage point to witness the marvels and moves of God.

41

I met Brother Anderson at Pisgah where we became great friends. Whenever I would see him, whether at church or at his home, Brother Anderson would see me coming a block away and would come bouncing down the street saying, "Well, Brother Tommy! I'm so glad to see you." And I was always glad to see him!

Brother Anderson had a medium build and shiny eyes that glowed. His slicked back, gray, balding hair accented his ruddy complexion. You could recognize him from afar off because of the bounce to his walk. Perhaps his most memorable characteristic was that he always had a beautiful smile on his face and was always bubbly and happy. In all the years I knew him, never once did I ever see him frown.

I had the privilege of going to Brother Anderson's home about once a month on Thursday evenings. I would be at least a block away when he would bounce out to meet me halfway and welcome me to his home. Unlike the ladies, Brother Anderson didn't have homemade cookies—his were store-bought—but he'd have cold milk and cookies waiting for me. I still remember the way he would dress. He would have on a plain, long-sleeved shirt buttoned all the way up including the top button and always tucked in. He wore slippers and regular slacks with a belt rather than suspenders. Out of respect, I would sit at his feet on a barren wooden floor as he settled into his vinyl-covered rocking chair. Perhaps "settled in" is not quite the way to describe this adventure. He didn't really sit in his chair; he would sit on the edge of it.

When he began to tell his stories, he would throw his hands up, bounce in his chair, and excitedly explain different miracles he had seen or prayed for at Azusa.

The image of Brother Anderson and his home live in my memory. Here is this old man, living in a sparsely decorated apartment, with few furnishings. One picture hanging on the wall that stood out was of John G. Lake and Brother Anderson side by side—a picture taken about sixty years earlier. Although his possessions were few, this man was rich in priceless memories and invaluable experiences that gold could never buy.

"Tell me again about your days at Azusa." I would begin the discussion and Brother Anderson would come to the edge of his chair and begin to bounce as he began his stories.

Many times he would begin with his own personal experience. Although he was born-again before attending Azusa, there he received the gift of speaking in tongues shortly after the revival began. He recalls that when he began to speak in tongues, he would do so in a loud voice, as if some one had turned up his volume. As soon as he blared out "tongues," to his amazement and shock, someone interpreted what he was saying. When recalling the entire experience, he would describe it as being in heaven. He longed to see another revival like Azusa.

From tongues to healings was a logical pro-gression. I always wanted to know about the miracles the Azusa Saints had been a part of. Brother Anderson told me that many who were blind and deaf were healed and that he was a part of many of those healings. Some were older people, some were middle age, and some were young—teenagers just like him. If he wasn't part of the miracle happening, he was most likely standing on a bench watching other miracles happen.

He told me that he was only about fifteen years old and had attended Azusa about ten times when God first used him in helping people receive healing. A young man, not much older than Brother Anderson, had a clubfoot and when he entered the meeting, he tried to hide his disfigurement. He explained to Brother Anderson that he didn't want people feeling sorry for him.

Brother Anderson asked the young man, "Are you aware of the Shekinah Glory? We are in the miracles of God. You don't have to have this." He went on to explain to the young man that Jesus, when He died on Calvary, got 39 stripes on His back, and they were for his healing.

The young man replied, "But that was for sickness and disease; I just have my foot turned sideways."

Brother Anderson replied, "God will heal it! You should see some of the miracles here."

The young man finally believed a miracle was possible, and Brother Anderson began to pray for him. To their astonishment, shortly after the prayer, the foot didn't just pop out, but rather it just started to slowly move outward. In a matter of minutes, the young man was jumping, running, and shouting. The foot had been deformed since he was a young child, and it had just gotten worse as he had gotten older. Yet, in just a few minutes, the foot was healed and perfectly formed.

Brother Anderson was right behind this young man dancing and shouting also. This may have been the first time God used Brother Anderson to work a miraculous healing through faith and prayer, but it was far from the last.

Brother Anderson recalls praying for a woman much older than him with a big knot just above her wrist. She didn't know what it was, but it hurt. When he asked her about the pain, she told him that she couldn't even work at home. Rather than lifting, she would scoot things with her arm. Brother Anderson told her that she didn't have to do that, because Jesus would heal her. He reached out, barely touched the knot and said, "In the Name of Jesus, be healed." In seconds, the knot was gone. Immediately, she got so excited that she started doing a dance right there on the spot, and Brother Anderson became her dance partner.

I was captivated by his stories. I asked him about the greatest or most unusual healing or miracle he had witnessed, and he told of a miracle that left me full of wonder. A younger woman named Diane, maybe in her late teens or early twenties, with two young children, walked into the revival meeting with her hand supporting a large growth or tumor about half the size of a basketball on the side of her head. She looked pitiful.

Before she could even get seated, people, including Brother Anderson, started surrounding her. Anderson told the woman that God was going to work a miracle for her. She kind of rolled her head and her eyes but didn't say a word. She came to get a miracle, and all she could do was nod her head "yes."

As the people began to lay hands on her, the tumor or growth began to shrink. The woman was speechless, standing there gasping and finally yelled "I'm Healed!"

Through the Grace of God, I got to meet Sister Diane while I was at Pisgah in the Sixties. She wasn't obese, but she wasn't a little woman. She stood just under six feet tall with a broad face and a marvelous spirit. I asked her about the healing, and here was what she shared with me. She had heard that things like miracles were happening at the Azusa Street Warehouse. She even saw the flames going up and coming down. So, she thought to herself, "What have I got to lose? I'm dying and if I go there, and I die, so what! The doctors can't do anything. They can't operate because it is too big to cut off."

"So," she says, "I waddled myself down to Azusa, holding my growth in my hands." A little embarrassed, she walked into the meeting and shortly after, the miracle happened. She remembered Brother Anderson being right in the middle of the miracle and just fell in love with him.

That miracle not only saved her life but propelled her into a ministry that would impact thousands of people over the years. With just 25 cents to her name, she started a soup kitchen when she was in her early twenties and was still serving soup to the needy and downtrodden when I met her.

Of course, I wanted to know more about Brother Seymour, and Brother Anderson was more than willing to oblige. He loved when Brother Seymour would come down to the service. Young Anderson would sit near him and try to peek under the box to see if Seymour was praying at all. He would lean as far down as possible to try to see, but he could never see under the box. Sometimes, Seymour would sit for ten minutes and sometimes for over an hour, doing nothing but sitting with the box over his head. During that time, Anderson would spend the same amount of time fascinated by the box and watching Brother Seymour to see even if his hands or feet moved. Young Anderson remembers that much like a statue, Seymour sat perfectly still during almost all of the time he was under the box.

Brother Anderson was in awe of Brother Seymour. He told me that Seymour was one of the sweetest men he had ever met. Tradition tells us that when Seymour got married to Jenny Moore, two women got upset because they felt he didn't have time for marriage with the return of Christ so eminent. These ladies got so upset that they stole his mailing list and ran off to Portland. That incident really upset young Anderson.

Anderson was so enamored of Seymour that he tried to imitate him. A few times he would get up and say, "Everybody in this section that needs healing stand up and be healed." Anderson learned very quickly that what

47

God had blessed Seymour with could not be duplicated except as God willed, so Anderson would go back to laying hands on those needing miracles.

Young Anderson believed that Seymour was a man of faith who never doubted anything. Every time he opened his mouth and said something, it happened. I learned from Brother Anderson that Seymour was a brilliant preacher. Anderson watched how Seymour spoke. Seymour would come out with phrases that were so intelligent and yet simple enough that the most uneducated could understand him. Anderson told me that the wisdom of this man was phenomenal.

The greatest thing that impressed Anderson was when the Spirit would fall on Seymour and he would start working the gifts. Anderson would get up on the benches so he could see Seymour talking to the people. There were quite a few times that there were people with what looked like rheumatoid arthritis, and Seymour would point to maybe a dozen of them and say, "You want to see a miracle over there? Everyone of you within a few minutes are going to be up and walking in the Name of Jesus." And every one of them—you could hear their bones popping—would be up shouting as their legs and arms and hands straightened out.

A few times Anderson witnessed Seymour perform one-on-one healings. One such healing stood out in Anderson's memory. A man whose face was deformed with small growths all over his face came to Brother Seymour. The deformed man looked very homely and ugly. Brother Seymour prayed for him, and immediately the growths began to fall off his face, restoring his face and making him whole. Perhaps the most stunning detail is that volunteers had to come and clean up those growths that had fallen from the man's face to the floor.

As long as Seymour was there, young Anderson didn't shout or dance. His eyes were totally focused on Seymour. Anderson confirmed that this power stayed with Seymour until the time he stopped placing the box over his head.

Anderson told me that when Seymour stopped putting the box on his head, it was the first time he was ever disappointed in the man. Anderson felt that Seymour had surrendered to the pressure of the people rather than staying obedient to God.

After talking about Seymour, the transition to the Shekinah Glory was logical. I asked Brother Anderson to describe what the Shekinah Glory was like, and he again brightened up as he came to the edge of his rocker.

Anderson told me that the Shekinah Glory was hard to explain because it could only be described, but not understood. At times, he would come into the building, and there would be kind of a glow. There were times that God would start moving and working, and a smoke-like substance would begin to glow even brighter. People could walk through it, and sometimes it would sort of roll. You couldn't take a fan and blow it out, nor was it something you could pick up. Brother Anderson confessed that he tried because it looked so tangible. He remembered that at times the mist would get so thick that it would fill the whole building. Anderson also noted that at times even Seymour was fascinated with the heavy mist that filled the room. In fact, there were times that Seymour would take his feet and kind of play with the thick Shekinah Glory.

Brother Anderson was awed by the Glory and described it as a part of heaven coming down. You could walk in it, sit down in it, run your hands through it, and breathe it into your lungs, but you could not capture it.

I pressed Brother Anderson to tell me about the "fire." Although he was not one of the first to go out and witness the event, he told me that he had seen it. He said it looked like flames about fifty feet in the air coming down and was also going up out of the roof to meet, merge, and go on through the flame coming down. Young Anderson would just stand there with his mouth open. He didn't know how to explain it, but it was real. He told me the burning bush described by Moses now made sense.

One event, confirmed by others, that Anderson noted was that whenever the people worshipped by singing in tongues, the power was greater. Every time this happened the anointing fell on the service.

Anderson was absolutely awed by the Shekinah Glory. One of the favorite songs sung by the Saints gathered at Pisgah was intricately linked with their encounter with God's Glory. The song that they sang with great enthusiasm was appropriately entitled, *Heaven Came Down and Glory Filled My Soul.*

Before the stories ended, I wanted to know about the other teenagers Anderson hung around with. Much like Sister Carney, Anderson also remembered both Ralph Riggs and C.W. Ward being a part of the group of young people who went around praying for people to be healed and being used by God to perform His miracles.

Anderson recalled a story about Ward that he thought was somewhat comical. Ward had a unique way of praying for somebody. He would swing his hips and go through all sorts of dramatic gestures. It was almost a theatrical production. He would do these big long prayers, swing his shoulders and hips, and yell out "In the Name of Jesus."

I asked Brother Anderson if God used Ward to bless others. Anderson would smile and say, "Well, they did get healed!" Ward was young just like the rest of them and was going through his teenage years. Although his actions may not have been orthodox, those years at Azusa prepared both Ward and Riggs to be used of God in mighty ways.

As I mentioned earlier, young Anderson also became good friends with John G. Lake. One of Anderson's prized possessions was the picture of Lake and himself that still hung on his living room wall some sixty years after Azusa.

The stories Brother Anderson told were firsthand accounts both of his observations of what transpired at Azusa and what he actually participated in during this great revival when he was just a teenager. His vivid recollection of the miracles and the Shekinah Glory that he witnessed validates the great outpouring of God's Spirit for over three years, beginning in 1906. Brother Anderson allowed me to experience Azusa through his eyes and captured for me the excitement and awe of this unprecedented revival.

My prayer echoes the prayer of Brother Anderson that someday soon we will experience the outpouring of God like during the days of Azusa.

WHEN MUSIC FILLED THE AIR

Meet Brother Sines and Brother Christopher
Azusa Ages: 26 and 18

Seymour was unpredictable. Once he took the box off his head, everyone knew that something was about to happen—they just never knew *what* was next. Many times Seymour would take the box off, get up and instruct the people to sing a certain song. The melodious sound of hundreds of people blending their voices was a bit of heaven. Seymour would sit and sing with them, his eyes closed as if the music itself were an offering to God.

Soon after the singing started, Seymour would instruct the people to "Sing in the Spirit." Whenever that happened, heaven itself came down and filled the room. The music was beyond description, pure yet powerful. This heavenly music became known as a "new song" as the crowd began to sing in a heavenly language, sometimes in tongues, sometimes without words. At times it seemed as if angels joined in the singing. "Singing in the Spirit" was a new song led by the Spirit of God.

Although singing in the Spirit was already a part of many of the services, when Brother Sines and Brother

Christopher became part of the leadership team, the heavenly music was enhanced. With the addition of piano and violin, the new heavenly song went beyond the ordinary to the extraordinary.

Brother Sines was about 26 years old when he came to the Azusa Revival in about 1907. He was a bit older than the youth we have been sharing about in this book but still quite young to be a part of the leadership team that led the services.

I met Sines at Pisgah in 1960. I stayed in a three-story men's dormitory where Sines was Dormitory Director for all the single men staying at Pisgah. He stood about five feet, nine inches tall, and was heavyset but not obese. When I met him, he walked stooped over a little bit but didn't use a cane. I can still see his receding hairline—about one-third of it gray—his dark eyes and a good–sized nose.

Like the others, I would go to Brother Sine's room about once a month. I would sit at his feet, and while munching on chocolate chip cookies and drinking some cold milk, listen to his stories about Azusa. He had a mild, pleasant voice and spoke softly.

Unlike the others, I had a deal with Sines that I would come and clean his apartment if he would tell me his stories. True to my word, I would first mop his floors with a dry mop and then with a wet mop. The floors were covered with linoleum so they were easy to clean. When I was finished, we would sit down and Sines would tell his stories.

A concert pianist, Brother Sines was all about music and fondly recalled his role in the music at Azusa. Seymour would lift the box from his head and often ask Sines to begin singing a certain hymn or song. At first, Sines would begin the song and lead the crowd in singing the request of Seymour. Later on, Sines brought his own piano to the meeting place and when he was instructed to sing, he would begin playing the song on his piano and leading the music. Without sheet music or a hymnal, whatever song Seymour wanted, Sines would sing and play the song from memory.

Sines recalled with joy the experience of singing in the Spirit. He remembered that virtually every time Seymour instructed them to "Sing in the Spirit," something wonderful and beyond understanding would happen. The music would rise to a new level, and the sound that came from Azusa was like a heavenly choir singing.

I asked Brother Sines about the miracles at Azusa and if he personally was ever involved in them. He would smile and in his soft voice, begin to share with me his first and favorite miracle. Seymour had not yet come down to the meeting. Sines was on the platform leading the crowd in songs when he saw a young crippled boy on crutches sitting off to the side unnoticed by those going about the crowd performing miracles. Sines came down from the platform, approached the young boy and asked him why no one was ministering to him. The little boy shrugged his shoulders with a kind of "I don't know" shrug and said, "I'm just waiting for someone to come over and pray for me." Sines asked the child, "Do you believe that God is going to heal you?" The boy, with a look of anticipation on his face, said, "Why, yes!"

Sines took the crutches from him, laid them down on the floor, and then laid hands on the boy and prayed for him. At first, nothing happened, but then the boy began to exclaim, "I feel it, I feel it," leaping to his feet, dancing, running, and shouting with Sines right behind him. Sines would tell me about other miracles, but none were so engraved in his memory as the joy of seeing this young crippled boy healed and so full of joy and thanksgiving.

Like many others, Sines was drawn to the power and anointing God had given Brother Seymour. Unlike others, Sines was on the platform with Seymour, and at least fifty percent of the time he was able to sit right next to him.

Brother Sines was obsessed with "the box." The reason he would try to sit next to Seymour whenever possible was so that he could get close enough to the box to see and hear what was going on inside. It did not matter if the box was on Seymour's head ten minutes or one hour, during that time, Sines could not pay attention to anything else, observing the box and Seymour the entire time. He would sit there thinking, "God, are You talking to this man or is he just sitting there waiting, listening or meditating?"

When Sines was out eating or fellowshipping with Seymour, he would ask him about what was going on in the box.   Seymour told him that he was meditating, waiting on God.   Seymour noted that when he would speak to God, he could hear himself talk, but it was always a whisper, and always in tongues.   When Sines asked Seymour if he understood what he was saying, Seymour responded that he knew what he had said, but he would hear himself say it in a different language—yet he still knew what he was saying.

Sines recalled that there was a glow around the box while it was on Seymour's head.   He observed the glow but told me he dared not touch Seymour or the box. He was afraid of what would happen.   He would lean over as close to the box as possible and just listen, but he would never get close enough to accidentally come in contact with the glow or the box.

We talked a little bit about what Sines observed from the platform, and he commented on young Ward's style and his silly facial expressions.   Sines recalled that Ward was comical to watch, but that God worked through him in a mighty way.   He also commented that Brother Anderson must have been kin to the kangaroos the way he bounced around.   He would watch Anderson get so excited that he would climb on a bench to see everything. He also noted that Sister Carney was the ringleader of it all.   She kind of directed the floor events.   By way of a side note, Sister Carney and Brother Sines were the best of friends and spent many hours in the gardens at Pisgah talking and reliving Azusa memories.

Brother Christopher, a young man around 18 years old, joined Sines about six months after coming to Azusa. I met Christopher while I was at Pisgah and actually lived with him at the dorm. I found him to be one of the politest men I'd ever known. He was a very small, frail man, weighing around 110 pounds, and standing about five feet, five inches tall. By the time I met him, he was in his seventies but still had a full head of coal black hair. He was somewhat dark-skinned and told us he was part Italian. Extremely shy and quiet, Brother Christopher didn't just talk; you had to pull it out of him.

He and Sines were great friends and played many concerts together. Christopher owned a Stradivarius violin and would bring it to Azusa to accompany Sines when he played the piano.

Like Sines, Christopher loved the music at Azusa and confirmed that the experience of singing in the Spirit was unequalled by anything he had ever experienced in his musical career. An accomplished concert violinist equaled by few, he would share with me that when he played in the spirit, he played at a level he'd never achieved even in his greatest concert.

Brother Christopher talked a little about the Shekinah Glory and told me that he even tried to bottle it. To his disappointment, there was nothing in the bottle the next day.

Brother Christopher was an observer. Because of his shyness, he didn't go out into the crowd. Those he was involved with when used by God for healing came up to him while he was on the platform. Christopher remarked that people must have thought he was someone important because he sat on the platform. I asked Brother Christopher, "Did anything happen to the people you prayed for?" He would quietly say with a smile, "Oh, yes, Brother Tommy, oh, yes."

He fondly told me about praying for a blind man whose wife had brought him to Azusa. The wife led her husband by his right hand—his white cane with the red tip in his other hand. She brought the man up to Christopher and said, "My husband is blind, heal him."

Christopher quietly said, "I can't heal him, but I can pray for him and Jesus will heal him."

She said somewhat demandingly, "Okay, do it!" Brother Christopher humbly and obediently prayed for the man and he was instantly healed.

I asked, "Didn't that excite you and make you want to do more?" Christopher replied, "Why, yes, I wished more would have come to me."

Brother Christopher told of a young man who had burned his arm at work. The arm was badly infected and green with gangrene. It was bad—so bad that Brother Christopher said that his arm should have been amputated. Christopher prayed for him and told him to go home and clean the wound because there were things working in his arm—bad stuff—and then bandage it. The man went home, cleaned and bandaged the burn, and came back the next night completely healed. Christopher was impressed with the man's willingness to be obedient to God's instructions and do what he was instructed to do. The following evening when the healed man returned, Brother Christopher rejoiced with him as they celebrated the awesome miracle from God.

Although Christopher only performed a few miracles because of his shyness, they were mighty works of God and bore witness that if you were at Azusa and your heart was right, God found a way to involve you in His miraculous works. If something like shyness kept you from going to the people, God in His marvelous ways would bring the people to you.

Many times while at Pisgah, I had the privilege of hearing Brother Sines play the piano and Brother Christopher play his violin. Sometimes my mind would wander. I would sit at Pisgah wondering what it must have been like to hear them play at Azusa when God's Spirit took the music to a heavenly realm as the people sang a new song in the Spirit. I believe that soon, we too will join a heavenly choir and be lifted to a new level of worship as we sing in a heavenly atmosphere as God's Spirit falls upon us.

I remember someone writing or saying that the music was like the very breath of God coming forth from human vocal cords. For now, I can only imagine!

MOTHER, BEHOLD THY SON

Meet Brother Riggs and Mom
Azusa Ages: 12 and 35

We have talked about how God used youth and young adults to manifest many of His miracles. In chapter after chapter, we find kids as young as twelve years old being used of God in a mighty way. What we haven't talked about are the parents of these children— how they felt and what they experienced as their children were so involved in the Azusa experience. This chapter takes a brief detour as we meet not only Ralph Riggs but also his mother.

I met "Mother" Riggs at Pisgah in 1960. I must confess that Mother Riggs made the best chocolate chip cookies, bar none, and she made them big and round.

When she was at Azusa watching her son run around and be used of God, she was in her late thirties. By the time I met her, she was in her nineties. She told me that she mainly watched "Ralphy" run around—a nickname that wasn't Ralph's favorite. Mother Riggs told me that Ralph and his best friend, C. W. Ward, didn't complain that they had to be at church. In fact, they preferred to be in church rather than anywhere else!

Don't misunderstand; Mother Riggs wasn't just a spectator. She too was actively involved in healings and miracles and spent much of her time with Sister Carney. Although she mainly participated with others, God also used her when she was by herself.

Mother Riggs had bright beady eyes that would just glow as she started talking about Azusa and they glowed as she told her story. She told me of her experience with about a dozen elderly people who reminded her of her parents. They were all brought to the meeting in wheelchairs and didn't have any major deformities or diseases. They were just old and feeble. She learned well from Sister Carney about expecting miracles, and if anybody in a wheelchair needed to be ministered to, she would put the footrests up before she prayed for the person. Immediately after the prayer, these frail, old people got up, hooked their arms together and began to dance. Sister Riggs was so thrilled to see old people up dancing and worshipping the Lord that she joined right in.

She told me that she also prayed for a man because he couldn't put any weight on his ankle due to the pain. Sister Riggs asked him, "Did you come to be healed?"

He told her, "Well, everybody is getting healed here they tell me. They just come and they get healed and I want my ankle healed."

She laid hands on his head and prayed for him. Within moments, the ankle that had been twisted popped and was healed. He stood up and began to dance and shout, and Mother Riggs just marveled at the miracle.

Like all the others, Mother Riggs loved the Shekinah Glory. She told me that the main thing she missed was the power of the mist or cloud as it glowed. She was convinced that the Glory they experienced was a part of heaven, and she was walking in it, living in it, and breathing it in.

She was also convinced that the abundance of miracles was happening because of the Shekinah Glory and the Presence of God in the meetings.

I loved her stories and I loved the fact that she not only supported her son, but she was right there with him as he enjoyed being used by God.

On occasion, Ralph Riggs would stop by Pisgah to visit with his mom. During four of those visits I had the honor of spending time with him. As mentioned earlier in this book, Ralph and C.W. Ward were instrumental in founding the Assemblies of God. Even though I knew he had stories in abundance about the Assemblies of God, I wanted to know about Azusa and his teenage years there.

Brother Riggs told me that he appreciated the fact that he wasn't just a spectator watching older people do miracles; God also used him to do them. He was given the liberty to go to anyone he wanted to and pray for them, and to his astonishment they all got healed. He worked with his best friend, C.W. Ward, who was two years his senior. Riggs noted that each of them had six or more miracles or healings every night. When it came to miracles, they weren't a team; it was every man for himself.

I asked Brother Riggs about the kids he hung around with at Azusa. He told me that Sister Carney was his favorite. He commented, "You kind of did what she told you to do. No one appointed her to be in charge, she just was a natural leader." Riggs also told me he loved to talk to and play with Brother Anderson, and of course there was Brother Ward, his best friend.

When I asked Brother Riggs about his most memorable miracles, he shared a few of his many, many experiences. His biggest miracle was this big, gawky guy, in his early twenties, who stood over six feet, five inches tall and weighed over 250 pounds. He came into the meeting with alcohol on his breath, slurring his words, and reeking of stale alcohol.

Riggs felt a voice inside of him saying, "Pray for him." Finally, Brother Riggs went over to the man, realized that not only had he been drinking but was also blind. Somewhat stunned, Riggs looked at him and said, "You can't see, can you?"

The man said, "No, that's what I came here for." Riggs, now somewhat more compassionate, prayed for him and he was instantly healed. Not only were his eyes healed, even the stench of alcohol was gone. The man just sat for a while crying and sobbing and finally said, "Well, it's true. It's true. I'm healed."

Here was a homeless, blind, alcoholic restored through the miraculous power of God, who later in life was used of God to preach revivals and establish many Pentecostal, and later on, Assemblies of God Churches across the Midwestern United States. Riggs noted that he had the privilege of visiting many of these churches in his travels with the Assemblies of God.

Brother Riggs also told of his one and only mass healing. A group of people came from a retirement home and had minor problems like aching joints. Riggs decided he would try a "Seymour" and have a mass healing. He looked at them and said, "Everyone of you are going to be healed in the Name of Jesus. Now, all of you be healed!" Unlike every other time he tried to mimic Seymour but it never worked, this time Riggs witnessed a mass healing, as the joints cracked and healed.

Although God used Brother Riggs in countless miracles, he chose to share only one last story. Two people, a husband and wife, came down in wheelchairs, pushed by their teenage children. They were both very sick and had either pneumonia or really bad colds.

Brother Ralph went over to them and asked, "Did you come down here tonight believing God is actually going to heal you?" The husband said, "Yes." Riggs began to pray for them, but he stopped suddenly as he remembered the "Carney Rule." He said to himself, "Sister Carney won't let me do that," and put up the footrests before finishing his prayer.

The stage was now set for God to work a miracle. Riggs got between the couple, placed his hands on their foreheads, and prayed, commanding them to be healed in the Name of Jesus. They both had had terrible fevers and the first thing Riggs noticed was that their temperatures had gone down. Within moments, the woman began to shake and shortly she was up and running. The man just stood up, raised his hands and screamed in a very loud voice, "Thank you, God; Thank you, God." God had healed them instantly.

Most of the time the Shekinah Glory was spoken of with reverence, but there was one time that Brother Riggs shared revealing a lighter side. He told me that when Seymour would get down there, the Shekinah Glory would get so thick that you could hardly see the ground. With a smile, he confessed that there were times when it was so thick that he and Ward would get in the back of the room and play hide-and-go-seek in the mist.

Since they were just young teenagers when at Azusa, I asked him if he ever tried to put Seymour's box on his head. He said with great reverence, "Nobody touched Seymour's box even when he wasn't down there. It was sacred."

I asked him to seriously talk to me about the Shekinah Glory. Brother Riggs explained the experience much like his mother. "I tasted a bit of heaven. Ward and I would talk and share that Azusa must have been what Heaven is like. God must have sent some part of heaven down here."

Mother Riggs and her son were a joy to talk to and to learn even more about the Azusa Revival. I met Ralph Riggs when he was in his seventies after God had used him mightily to advance His Kingdom. After talking with Brother Riggs, my mind would wander back to his days at Azusa. I could see him running around full of life as he and other teenagers and young people were involved in the awesome outpouring of God. Instead of waiting until he was older to begin his ministry, by the time he reached adulthood, he had already been used of God in a way that most adults—especially in their twilight years—only dream about.

Azusa Youth Tell Their Stories

THE TOPEKA CONNECTION

Meet Mr. And Mrs. Lankford

Azusa Ages: 20 and 18

Three years before the Azusa Revival there was Topeka, Kansas. In 1903, Dr. Charles Parham had started a Bible School in Topeka where he taught about the Baptism of the Holy Spirit accompanied by the gift of tongues, which he personally had experienced.

In 1903, a young man of seventeen, Brother Lankford, was led of God to leave Highland Park, California, and travel to Topeka to learn about this new teaching. Under Parham's witness, he received the Baptism and gift himself. Little did Lankford understand the significance of his venture to Kansas.

He returned to California in 1904 and introduced this new teaching to Dr. Yoakum, the founder of Pisgah. Dr. Yoakum, after receiving the Baptism and gift of tongues, in turn, taught others at Pisgah about this exciting experience. You will recall that it was because of Brother Lankford and Dr. Yoakum that Sister Carney received the Baptism and gift in 1904, two years prior to Azusa.

Azusa was not an after-thought of God. This great visitation of God was ordained long before the actual experience took place. The prayers offered the past several years that focused on seeking revival were but the final stage of this God-ordained experience. Even before the first prayer was offered, God was preparing many people to participate in this magnificent outpouring of His Spirit.

One such Saint was Brother Lankford, who had a hunger to know all that he could about yielding himself to God. This desire led him to Topeka, then back to California, and eventually to Azusa where he would be used of God in mighty ways. According to Mrs. Lankford, he was personally involved in over 100 miracles and healings.

I had the privilege of getting to know Brother Lankford and his wife during my time at Pisgah. He was a few inches taller than six feet, and she stood about five-ten. Mrs. Lankford was a good-sized lady who was soft-spoken and very sweet. On the other hand, Brother Lankford was tall and slender but gruff at times.

Unlike my other visits, when I came to their home, I wasn't greeted with cookies and milk. Brother Lankford had discovered my weakness for strawberry ice cream, which was also his favorite. So I sat at their feet and enjoyed ice cream while listening to their stories.

The Lankfords were all about being used by God to bring about healings and miracles. When we talked, the entire evening was one story after another about the miraculous works of God at Azusa.

I would often begin by asking the Lankford's to tell me their most interesting miracles. Once the question left my lips, there was no turning back. Brother Lankford would begin and Mrs. Lankford would add her memories to those of her husband.

"I witnessed a man's fingers actually grow back." That statement would grasp my attention as I begged for more details. Lankford told me about a man who had gotten two fingers caught several weeks earlier in some type of machine, and before he knew it the machine had ripped off two of his fingers. The man had heard that astonishing miracles happened at the Azusa Warehouse, so he came with the expectation of getting healed.

Brother Lankford shocked the man by asking, "Can we see what God will do?"

The man, somewhat puzzled, replied, "What do you mean?"

"Let's ask God to grow them out!" Lankford was very bold and outspoken. With the man's approval, Lankford grabbed the man's hand and instructed him to put it up in the air. Holding the man's hand up high, and with Sister Lankford holding his arm, Lankford began to pray. As soon as the man's fingers began to grow out, Sister Lankford passed out from the sight of such a miracle. As Brother Lankford held firmly to the man's hand, they watched the miracle happen before their very eyes!

Lankford started taking the man around shouting that his fingers had just grown out. You could hear

71

Lankford cry out, "These weren't here before. Look, God grew these fingers out." The man stood next to Lankford in shock with his mouth open in amazement. Before the miracle was over, even the man's fingernails grew out as the man was made whole.

Mrs. Lankford smiled as her husband told about the greatest miracle he had been a part of and as soon as he finished, she said, "Let me tell you my most memorable miracle."

Sister Lankford didn't wait for approval and began to tell about her story. At the time of this miracle, the Lankfords were engaged, and she said somewhat forcefully, "Honey, come here!"—He wasn't used to her talking like that because she was very sweet and very soft-spoken. She said, "Look here at this sister of ours that God is going to heal."

The lady had a very bad hunchback. Her back didn't just curve over; it was twisted. She was an older woman, probably around 50 to 55 years old. She told Sister Lankford that the problem had started when she was about 30, and it had just gotten worse and worse. The doctor wanted to put her into a nursing home, and even her husband felt that she should be there because she could hardly get around. Well, her husband brought her, thinking that maybe God would do something at the revival meeting. Brother Lankford came over and laid his hands on the hunched back and started praying for her. You could hear the popping of the bones. Within minutes, right before their eyes, she was healed. She broke into dancing and even went up onto the platform dancing and screaming. Right behind her was Brother Anderson, who had been standing up on a bench where he saw the miracle happen and also could hear the bones cracking.

I asked Sister Langford, "What did you and Brother Langford do?'"

She responded, "Well, we were both running with her."

"You mean you were dancing?"

She smiled and said, "That was a long time ago, Brother Tommy."

I smiled and just said, "Oh."

Now it was Brother Lankford's turn. "Another memorable miracle is the crippled man in a wheelchair who wouldn't let the doctors cut off his legs." Lankford went on to explain that the man had worked as a brakeman for the railroad and had been crippled in an accident when a train pinned his legs down and broke many of his bones. You could tell through his pant legs that the bones in his legs were kind of knotty, but he was too shy or embarrassed to pull up his pant legs to show his injuries.

The Lankfords came up to this man, and Brother Lankford asked, "Well, what happened to you?" The man explained why he was confined to a wheelchair. Brother Lankford replied, "Well, we can't allow that to happen, it's about time you came here."

The man quietly said, "Yeah, I'm sorry, yes, I'm here." Lankford said that he wasn't sure if he had come alone, but he had pushed himself into the service.

When Brother Lankford saw him sitting there, he said it brought him to tears. He said to the man, "It's a miracle they didn't cut your legs off."

The crippled man answered, "I have been paralyzed from the waist down like this for about 2 years. They wanted to amputate, but I wouldn't let them."

Brother Lankford started praying for him, and Sister Carney, who was observing, broke in and corrected him. "No, no, no, that's not faith!" She went over to the man and picked up his legs and put the footrests up, so he could get up. She expected him to get up! After Sister Carney was done, Brother Lankford prayed for the man. You could hear the bones cracking and see the legs just straighten up. The man got out of his wheelchair and went flying—and of course, a bunch of those who surrounded the man went with him.

I thought that was an extreme phenomenon, and I asked Brother Lankford, "Did God have to put the bones back together?"

Lankford nodded and said, "Yes, God had to put the bones back together. You could see when the man came to Azusa that he was pathetic—he couldn't walk, and he couldn't move from the waist down. And here this man was running around the place shouting and dancing and leaping."

I sat there and would think, "It is no wonder they had such a revival, no wonder this thing went worldwide. Yes, they received the speaking in tongues and that was great, but many of the miracles that were performed were not done by big preachers. Many of those being used by God were just ordinary teenagers and young people doing extraordinary works through God."

Brother Lankford also was blessed with the great gift of helping those people that had cleft palates or lips to receive healing. Some of those who came there for healing had never had operations or medical treatment. There would be big gaps in their mouths and he would pray for them and the gaps would be filled in. Sometimes some of their teeth would be gone and the teeth would be restored.

I said, "Teeth and all?"

Brother Lankford nodded, and said, "Teeth and all."

Lankford said that over the three-year period he was there, God used him in healing around 100 people, many with cleft palates.

Mrs. Lankford wanted to continue with more stories, but Brother Lankford wasn't quite finished. "Two more stories. Let me tell you about the tumor on the spine. Even though the tumor was covered by the man's shirt, you could see the outline of the tumor. It stood out about 3 inches, and was about a foot long, and 4 inches wide." Brother Lankford described the man as middle-aged and according to him, had had the tumor for about 3 years. The man came in with a bunch of people, and someone let Brother Lankford know about him and that the next day he was to have x-rays taken to find out what was wrong. Lankford told how he prayed over the tumor and it just sunk into this body — the man was totally healed.

Without taking a breath, Brother Lankford went on to the next miracle. There was a woman with part of her nose gone from cancer. He prayed for her, but nothing happened immediately. He told the lady that sometimes miracles don't happen instantly and to have faith. She came back the next night and her nose was perfect.

Now it was finally Sister Lankford's turn again. She told about the time four or five blind people were brought in from a home for the blind. Sister Lankford walked up to them and announced that God was going to work miracles. Brother Lankford ran over to them, covered their eyes, and prayed for them, laying hands on each of them. Every time he removed his hands the results were the same: they could see! Instant healings! The whole place erupted in shouting and dancing.

I broke in and asked Sister Lankford if they had ever seen or participated in miracles where limbs or body parts were actually re-grown. They both confirmed that personally they only participated in the miracle where the man's fingers were restored but that such miracles did happen through Brother Seymour as he was anointed by God.

I asked if they remembered any specific miracles where God used Brother Seymour, and Sister Lankford's eyes lit up. "I recall witnessing two of the greatest miracles where Seymour was greatly used by God."

I was all ears! First, she told about the man with the wooden leg. Seymour had approached a man with a wooden leg and asked, "What did you come here for?"

The man replied, "I want you to pray for my leg. It is starting to get gangrene where the wooden leg attaches."

Seymour replied, "I'm just upset because you have the wooden leg on. It would be a challenge for God to grow a leg out when the wooden leg is attached."

The man removed the wooden leg and stood before Seymour standing on his one good leg. Seymour laid hands on the man and proclaimed, "Let Thy Name be Glorified. In the Name of Jesus, I command this leg to grow out. The gangrene is gone; you are healed." Seymour didn't preach that night. The miracle spoke for itself. Rejoicing was continuous as the crowd went wild. The man ran upon the platform and around the room. No one could get him to stop rejoicing and praising God.

Next, Sister Lankford told of the man with *no* arm. Seymour spoke with a man who had lost his arm ten years earlier through a work-related accident. The arm had been totally severed at the shoulder.

Brother Seymour asked the crowd, "Would you like to see God have a wonderful time here tonight? Some of you may remember the man's leg that grew out about a year ago."

Seymour then asked the one-armed man, "Can you work with just the one arm?"

"I'm just given minimal paying jobs and I barely make enough money to even eat."

Seymour shook his head and responded, "That's not good. Are you married?"

"Yes."

"Got kids?"

"Yes."

"This man needs to be able to make a living. This man needs to work and he needs to be able to pay his tithe. Will you tithe if I pray for you and God gives you your arm back?" Seymour said teasingly.

"Yes!"

Seymour burst out laughing. "I'm just having fun." He then slapped his hands on the shoulder itself and commanded the arm to grow out. Almost instantly it grew out. The healed man stood in total shock, then started moving his arm and feeling of it with his other hand, awed by the miracle.

A few weeks later the man came back, bringing about 200 people with him, telling many at the meeting that he had gotten his old job back. Many of those he brought with him needed healing and left that evening fully restored as people in the crowd prayed and laid hands on each of them.

As always, time passed quickly at the Lankford's home. The evening always ended too soon. As I would walk to my dorm room, I would relive the stories in my mind, marveling at the mighty works that the Azusa Saints witnessed and participated in. I longed for the day that the Shekinah Glory would fall again—and this time I wanted to be right in the middle of it.

Azusa Youth Tell Their Stories

LIVING PROOF

Meet Sister Mangrum
Azusa Age: 22

Remember these inspiring words from the song, "I Believe In Miracles"?

Creation shows the power of God, there's glory all around. And those who see must stand in awe, for miracles abound. I believe in miracles, I've seen a soul set free. Miraculous the change in one redeemed through Calvary. I've seen the lily push its way up through the stubborn sod. I believe in miracles for I believe in God.

This is a book about miracles—great miracles as recalled by faithful Saints of God who were eyewitnesses to the miraculous. Only the fool can say in his heart that God is not a God of wonder-working power, not only transforming lives on the inside, but often bringing healing and miracles for those who need Him to touch them in a special way.

Many of the Saints at Pisgah only had the memories of God's mighty, wonder-working power at Azusa, but that wasn't true for all of them. One such

Saint had living proof of God's power near her even when I met her at Pisgah. You see, I not only got to meet Sister Mangrum, I also got to meet a Saint that had been miraculously healed through the ministry of Sister Mangrum when she was at Azusa. Living there at Pisgah were both the one who was used of God to perform a miracle and the one who had received this miracle of healing. Since the lady that was healed was in her mid-forties at the time of the healing, I considered it a privilege that I got to meet her as she neared her hundredth birthday.

"Mother" Mangrum, as she was later called, was in her early twenties at Azusa but in her mid-seventies when I met her at Pisgah. She stood around five feet, two inches, and weighed about 110 pounds. She was always very well dressed, very prim and proper, well spoken, as well as kind and courteous.

Mother Mangrum often called me her "little" boy, and I had the honor of going once a month to her home, which was one of the larger apartments on the grounds. As tradition would dictate, she would bake chocolate chip cookies and serve cold milk during our time together. I sat on a big huge throw rug that almost covered the entire floor. She sat on a good-sized, antique, wooden rocking chair that had belonged to her great-grandmother. Mother Mangrum was part of the "Carney" crowd, and like Sister Carney, was married at the time of Azusa and attended the revival services with her husband.

One of Mother Mangrum's favorite stories was about the pigeon-toed woman. She was in her mid-forties and couldn't walk very well as her knees bowed inward and had been that way since her teenage years. Mother Mangrum immediately noticed her as she came scooting and wobbling in, walking kind of funny. Mother Mangrum went over to her and asked, "Have you come to be healed?"

The lady responded, "I came to see what was going on. You say I can be healed? Of What?"

Mother Mangrum pointed to her legs and said, "Of your legs." She sat down with the woman and tried to convince her that God would straighten up her legs.

The woman responded in a slight stutter, "Well, ah, ah, it's worth a try." She told Mother Mangrum that people had made fun of her a lot since she was a child.

Mother Mangrum eagerly responded, "Yes, what have you got to lose." She prayed for her, keeping her hands on the woman's head. She explained that it was kind of like heat coming out of her hands onto the woman. Finally the woman started shaking and said, "Something's happening, something's happening!"

Mother Mangrum looked down at the woman's legs and excitedly told the woman to look. Her feet and legs were straightening out, and in about two minutes, she was completely restored. Knees, twisted legs, and pigeon-toed feet were totally straightened and healed.

She asked the woman, "Would you like to walk normal now? We could do a dance all over this place."

She looked at Mother Mangrum and said, "I have never danced in my whole life."

Mother Mangrum smiled and said, "Well, let's learn now," and began to dance with her.

Soon, the woman realized that a miracle had really happened to her and went "wild" dancing before God Before Mother Mangrum knew it, the lady had run out of the building and several minutes later came running back in screaming and hollering—she wanted to get back into the building, afraid she might lose her healing if she wasn't inside. After she settled down, she looked around and asked, "What is this stuff?"

"We call it the Shekinah Glory."

While at Pisgah, I got to meet this lady, who by then was near 100 years old. For years she operated a rescue mission down on skid row for homeless women on the streets. After the miracle, she gave the rest of her life to ministering to homeless women. When I would go to see her, she was all but on her deathbed. Her one question to me and all the Saints was, "I just want to know what happened to that Shekinah Glory."

Of course, my curiosity got the best of me, and I asked to see this elderly woman's legs that had been healed. At first she was reluctant, but then with some encouragement from Mother Mangrum, she showed me her legs—still completely healed after all those years. She was living proof right before my eyes that God had visited Azusa in a mighty way.

Mother Mangrum always shared one other story. It was about the woman with the hooked nose. When she first noticed the lady, Mother Mangrum told me she thought that maybe a doctor could help fix her ugly nose, but God had other ideas. She heard a small voice within her say, "I am a better doctor than any doctor here on earth." With that message from God, she looked at the lady again and felt that she needed to pray for her.

She went to the woman and prayed, but the results were not immediate. Later on in the service, Mother Mangrum noticed that the "hook" was gone and went up to her and commented about the healing.

The woman was somewhat happy but told Mother Mangrum, "I know the hook is gone, but I don't like the little point at the end of my nose." Mother Mangrum understood her concern and prayed for her again, and before the lady left the meeting a few hours later, she had a *perfect* nose. Looking at God's miracle, Mother Mangrum silently rejoiced as she thought how wonderful it was that God even cared enough about a person's feelings to straighten out this lady's ugly nose.

Mother Mangrum was somewhat theatrical when she told her stories, and with many gestures made the stories come alive. Although I was impressed with what God had done back at the turn of the century, I knew that not far from where we were, there was a lady in her late nineties who was living proof.

Azusa Youth Tell Their Stories

A DIFFERENT CLAIM TO FAME
Meet Sisters Lucille and Laura
Azusa Ages: 18 and 16

In the 1950's, Lucille had a small claim to fame. Lucille Ball had made Lucille McGillicuddy's name famous by paying handsomely to use it as the maiden name of her television character in *I Love Lucy*. But her name is not all that she is remembered for. In fact, Lucille McGillicuddy made quite a name for herself by becoming the secretary for Aimee Semple-McPherson and her successor, Jean Darnall. In addition, she was part of the youth group that impacted the lives of many during the Azusa Street Revival.

I met Sister Lucille at Pisgah. She couldn't have weighed much more than 90 pounds and stood under five feet tall. She was very slender and petite. Like many of the Pentecostal women of that day, she had long hair that almost touched the floor but wore it in a glory bun held together by a host of hairpins.

Since she was one of the Azusa Saints, I had the honor of sitting down at her feet and listening to her recount her Azusa days. Yes, she made homemade chocolate chip cookies and always had a cold glass of milk waiting for me.

During her Azusa days, she was part of the Carney-Riggs-Ward-Anderson group and was instrumental in helping many receive healing. I would begin our time together by asking her to tell me about the greatest healing or miracle in which she personally participated. She always told of two miracles that were a vivid part of her memory.

First, she told me about the lady who had one leg shorter than the other. Her name was Goldie, and she had polio, causing one leg to be over four inches shorter than the other. Sister Lucille kept insisting that Goldie take the brace off and allow God to heal her. Goldie told Lucille, "If I take the brace off, I better be healed."

Sister Lucille smiled and said, "You will be! Now take it off." She took off the brace, and Sister Lucille immediately prayed for her. As Goldie and Lucille sat there, the leg straightened up. Lucille told her to get up and walk. She took her first steps and almost fell over because she was not accustomed to walking with normal legs—miraculously both legs were the same length.

Next, with a twinkle in her eye, she would tell me about the woman who had had her wrist shattered in a domestic squabble. The woman couldn't use her hand at all. Sister Lucille said, "It looks like your wrist has been crushed!"

She responded, "My husband hit it with a mallet. He was mad at me and thought he would teach me a lesson and crushed my wrist."

Sister Lucille told me that it just broke her heart. She earnestly wanted the lady healed and when she prayed, she all but begged God to heal her. After her prayer, she said to the wrist, "I say in the Name of Jesus, you do what I told you and be healed!" Immediately, the lady's wrist was totally restored.

Sister Lucille's next story was not a cookies and milk story. She would tell about the miracles performed on people who had very bad teeth, and usually I would lose my appetite. Lucille would have them open their mouths, and she would stick her fingers on the teeth that were bad and pray for healing. I asked her, "Were they infected and filled with bad stuff?" She would look at me with a half-grin on her face. I said, "You stuck your finger on their teeth?"

With that half-grin on her face, she said, "Yeah."

"What if there wasn't a tooth there?" I would ask playfully.

Sister Lucille took her story over the top. "I would stick my finger on the bare gum. In fact, many times I would push against the gum and let the new tooth push my finger out. On the really decayed teeth, all the bad stuff would come out, and we would use a handkerchief to rub the bad stuff off and there would be a new tooth. Even crooked teeth would straighten up."

I just sat there shaking my head. Even though her descriptions of the teeth often caused my stomach to turn, I sat in awe at the miracles she described.

She would ask me, "Tommy, wouldn't you love to see those kind of healings in our services today?" I would just nod in agreement.

What impressed Sister Lucille was that the miracles were not confined to Brother Seymour. She would comment, "A little bitty woman like me could walk up and command a leg to grow out, and it would grow out. A busted wrist would grow back together. Rotten teeth would be replaced with brand new teeth, and missing teeth would grow back in."

I asked her if she ever worked with someone who had all their teeth missing. She said "No, I never tried that."

I teasingly said, "Well, you should have."

She rebukingly replied, "I just never tried that Brother Tommy."

I would meekly change the subject and ask her to describe what the Shekinah Glory was like. She would get such joy in her eyes as she told me how much she loved to be in the center of the mist-like cloud. She was so little, she would sit down in it—when it was thick, the mist was about up to her neck. Like a kid, she would have fun and play in the mist. She would often lie down, breathing in the mist. She would tell how she could feel the energy of it and described that it was like being put into an oxygen tent.

When Brother Seymour was there, and they would sing in the Spirit, Sister Lucille told me that the Shekinah Glory would just rise and fill the whole room, and you could breathe so much better—as if the room were filled with pure oxygen.

Sister Lucille had a best friend, Laura Langtroff, who moved to Pisgah in 1955. Sister Laura became a part of Azusa when Lucille invited her to attend the revival.

When I met Sister Laura at Pisgah, she was in her seventies, stood about five feet, seven inches tall, and weighed around 170 pounds. She had dark brown, very long hair and kept it up in a glory bun. Sister Laura came from a very well-to-do family and was a wealthy woman in her own right, but she chose to live at Pisgah with her Azusa friends.

When I would talk to Sister Laura, she would tell me about Azusa through her eyes. She and Lucille both worked with a lot of people who had trouble breathing. They loved ministering to women and especially those who were old and feeble. Legend has it that if a woman came in with a cane or crutches and got near Sister Laura, she would be healed and walked away from the meeting, free of canes or crutches.

I remember asking Sister Laura, How many miracles or healings did you participate in?

She thought for a moment. "I attended every night, and there were at least three or four a night!"

Not long into our talk, I would ask the same question of Sister Laura that I asked of every Saint:

"What was the greatest miracle or healing you personally were a part of?" Sister Laura would tell me about one of the most exciting miracles she was involved in—and one of the most exciting miracles ever at Azusa.

Here's her story. A woman came into the meeting holding a staff. She could hardly breathe and looked like a skeleton. She only lived about two miles from Azusa and had started walking to Azusa about three in the afternoon but didn't reach the Warehouse until six in the evening. She literally took one baby step at a time, placing the staff in front of her then scooting her feet up to it and repeating the slow, tedious process until she reached the revival meeting. She reminded me of the woman in the Bible* who knew that if she just touched the hem of the garment of Jesus she would be healed. That evening at Azusa, this woman was determined to get healed. She came in, and looked around as if she were studying the room. At some point, her eyes met Laura's and she said, "That's the woman I want to pray for me," pointing to Sister Laura.

Sister Laura walked over to her and said, "Mother, what can I do for you?"

The next words the lady spoke were almost haunting. "I won't live through the night if God doesn't heal me; I'll die. Doctors say my lungs are ate up with cancer, and I can hardly breath. I've been losing weight for about a year."

This dear, feeble, elderly woman weighed about 65 pounds, standing at about five feet, six inches tall. She was nothing but bones. Sister Laura laid hands on her and prayed for her. Immediately, she was able to breathe normally. In the next three hours she would gain about 40 pounds while at the meeting, yet she ate nothing and only breathed in the Shekinah Glory. She said, "My lungs are not hurting; I can breathe like when I was young!"

Yes, there was a great celebration that evening. Sister Laura was a shouter. Her glory bun shook loose and hairpins flew everywhere as she celebrated with this dear Saint.

But that's not the end of the story. This lady went to her doctor—Thomas White, who later founded *Wings of Healing*. When she went to his office, he asked her if she had filled out the forms that first-time patients had to fill out—he did not recognize her. When she told him who she was, he could not believe she was the same person.

After running some tests and checking her out, he told her that her insides were just like new—lungs and all. In amazement, he told her, "There is no way you could have gained that much weight back since the last time I saw you. It is impossible!"

She boldly replied, "I know I couldn't, but God could."

The doctor exclaimed, "You're going down to that warehouse, aren't you?"

After attending the revival with her, in a few months, he was no longer practicing traditional medicine! He founded *Wings of Healing* where he experienced miracles galore. He told the Saints at Azusa that the woman cured of cancer and lung failure should have died six months earlier. Truly, her faith not only made her whole but also sustained her on her determined journey to find God and His miraculous power waiting for her at Azusa.

Sister Lucille and Sister Laura, both very wealthy, found something at Azusa money couldn't buy. They found a common bond forged by the mighty acts of God during Azusa. That bonded friendship was still strong and unbreakable sixty years later as these Saints fellowshipped with others who were touched by the Shekinah Glory poured out at Azusa.

Oh, dear God, find us worthy and allow Your Spirit to fall fresh on us with a new outpouring of Your Glory.

* Matthew 9:20

A LIFETIME OF MIRACLES

Meet Brother Cantrell

Azusa Age: 21

A myriad of Miracles happened at Azusa daily as people by the hundreds experienced the mighty power of God. Many understood that the miracles were a part of a unique visitation of God and were a direct manifestation of His Glorious Presence. One of the sad commentaries on the Azusa Street Experience is that many who were being used of God daily to perform miracles and healings rarely were ever used again for such mighty works.

Miracles were not unique to Azusa. They happened before Azusa and didn't end after Azusa. Some of the Saints of Azusa continued to be used of God to perform miracles their entire lives.

One man God continued to use was Brother Cantrell. I personally experienced two miracles from his hands that changed my life completely. It was Brother Cantrell who miraculously caused me to quit smoking and prayed for me for "holy boldness" that gave me the ability to speak in front of a large number of people—a gift that I certainly didn't have before he ministered to me.

Brother Cantrell was somewhat tall, standing five feet, nine inches. I vividly recall that he wore a hat all the time except when he was in church. Even though he was single, he baked fresh cookies and always had cold milk waiting for me for our long talks. Once a month I would go to his apartment, which was caddy-corner from Pisgah. When he told me his stories, I sat at Brother Cantrell's feet on a throw rug, and he sat in an upholstered chair.

Even when he told his stories, he never showed much emotion. He was pleasant, nice, and friendly but not big on emotions.

When our meetings first started, I asked him if he personally had had any great miracles. He replied, "Anyone who attended Azusa very long had great miracles—especially if a person attended at least once a week— you had miracles!"

"In fact," Brother Cantrell said, "God taught me a valuable lesson at Azusa. There was a man there who started quacking like a duck after receiving the Baptism of the Holy Spirit. I thought that the man was making a mockery of the Baptism and got upset with him. I thought, 'This is not a language.'

"Many years later in the 1930's, I saw a documentary about a tribe in a place called Quackland. Their language was just like that of a duck. I realized that I was upset with this poor man and all he did was speak in the language of Quackland. I have learned since never to question the acts of God, no matter how unique the act is."

I smiled at the story and asked Brother Cantrell to tell me about his most interesting miracle. He sat almost emotionless and told the story of the man who was what Cantrell called "tongue-tied." The man was in his late twenties, and instead of talking, he just mumbled. Brother Cantrell couldn't understand a word he said and finally told the man, "Let's stop talking and get you healed first so I can understand you."

The man nodded his head and Brother Cantrell laid hands on him and told him to stick his tongue out. The man gestured that he couldn't, so Brother Cantrell reached down in the man's mouth and touched his tongue. In an authoritative voice, he commanded, "In the Name of Jesus, tongue, I command you to be free." And miraculously he was able to stick his tongue out. Brother Cantrell looked at the man's tongue, now loosed, and asked the man, "Can you talk now?"

The man said, "I don't know." Then he realized that he was talking in a normal voice and got all excited. He ran shouting, "Glory, hallelujah!" He could speak perfectly. He didn't have to learn how to talk; he just needed his tongue loosed.

Brother Cantrell was personally involved in one or two miracles a week, but he observed thousands of miracles performed over the years. He was just about 20 years old himself but told me that he loved to watch teenagers like Riggs, Ward, Anderson, and Carney. They would be running around having an exciting time, smiles on their faces, and praying for people as God supernaturally worked miracles through them.

When the subject turned to Brother Seymour, Brother Cantrell told me that he stood in awe of him. He was impressed that what people thought did not influence Seymour. Brother Seymour had such an anointing that Cantrell stood back in awe, especially when Seymour participated in the leg and arm growing out.

Brother Cantrell was a man who was quiet and not given to much emotion, but continued even when I knew him to be used mightily of God. I loved his stories, but they were even more powerful when told by a man who continued to live out a small portion of Azusa even sixty years later.

CROSSING RACIAL BARRIERS

Meet Brother Garcia

Azusa Age: 18

Of all the stories told about Azusa Street, perhaps the most astonishing is that it was the first totally integrated Church in America. All barriers were broken as all races worshipped together as one, regardless of color, nationality, or creed. Those who gathered for over three years were truly one in the Spirit. When Seymour came down to the meeting, if he saw that the people had segregated themselves into racial groups, he would insist that they integrate.

Such an openness of worship and acceptance of every person regardless of race was one of the critical factors that led David Garcia, a young Mexican-American, to attend services at Azusa every evening after work as well as Saturdays and Sundays.

I met Brother David at Pisgah where he had lived since about 1955. He stood five feet and seven inches tall and weighed about 200 pounds. At the time of Azusa, David was around 18 years old and lived just about a mile from the Warehouse. He began attending the revival shortly after the meetings began in 1906.

99

When we got together to talk about Azusa, Brother Garcia broke tradition and served strong coffee rather than milk and cookies. That was basically the only difference as I sat at his feet in respect and listened to him re-live his memories of God's mighty works.

The story Brother David began with was the Grand Central Station experience. David lived about a half a mile on the other side of Grand Central Station and walked right by it coming to the Azusa Street Warehouse. One evening he ran to the meeting to find Frank Bartleman and told him that he needed to come to Grand Central Station.

"Why? What's going on there?" Bartleman asked out of curiosity.

Brother Garcia, while trying to catch his breath, exclaimed, "You've got to come and see this! The anointing is far beyond where it had been in the past. You have to come on down and see!"

Together Bartleman and Garcia ran down to the station that was a half-mile away from the Warehouse. There they witnessed people come in from all over the world, get off the train, walk across the platform, and fall out in the Spirit often speaking in tongues—Someone had commented that the phenomenon had been happening all day long.

When Garcia first saw the people laying all over the platform area, he thought it was a disaster until he realized what was going on and ran to find Bartleman. Frank had talked about a line or circle of blood—several blocks around the Azusa Warehouse—where the power of God extended outward. Several blocks before reaching the Warehouse, people were being healed, falling out in the Spirit,and speaking in tongues for the first time. This was the first time God's power had reached all the way to Grand Central Station. Although no miracles were taking place, the Presence and power of God, without question, had now moved out a half-mile from the actual warehouse!

Brother Garcia was awe struck by the Shekinah Glory that lingered for over three years at and around the Warehouse. He would tell me, "We have got to get the Shekinah back if we want to see a worldwide revival!"

I asked Brother David, "Did you ever see the flame?" He told that there were times he was coming to the meeting late and would see the flames as far away as Grand Central Station. Brother Garcia would think, "Whoo, God's moving again," and would run to Azusa because he knew that when the fire was falling, there was more power at the meeting and he wanted to be a part of it. He explained that the experience was greater than breathing pure oxygen. There were times the Shekinah Glory was only a foot high, and he would lie down in it to breathe God's Glory.

He often stressed that the greater the Shekinah Glory, the greater the power. He would note that the flames were there when God, through Seymour, per- formed the miracles where a leg re-grew and another where an arm re-grew.

Garcia was there when the arm grew out. He said, "Brother Tommy, he didn't have a ball joint in his shoulder, it had been ripped out of there. I was close enough to be looking right at the shoulder, and all of a sudden I saw the bones start to come out and then flesh started coming around them. His arm just shot out in what seemed mere seconds as I watched." For Garcia, it seemed like he was watching in slow motion as he was awed at what God was doing.

Brother Garcia was the first to tell me of Seymour's prophesy that in about 100 years there would be a return of the Shekinah Glory and a revival that would surpass the Works of God at Azusa.* When we talked in the Sixties, Garcia realized that the prophesy was still forty years away from being fulfilled, but still longed for God to accelerate His plans and allow the Shekinah Glory to fall again in his lifetime.

I loved to hear about the cloud or mist that filled Azusa signifying the Presence of God. I also loved to hear about the great miracles that happened in that mist. I would ask Brother David to describe the greatest miracle he had ever participated in. Without hesitation, he would tell of the multiple healings that took place all within a few minutes. There were two women and a man all with crippling arthritis and couldn't walk. They were in wheelchairs and had come from a nearby nursing home. One of the women couldn't even feed herself. Brother Garcia asked, "Did you come to get healed?" All three responded "yes" or nodded their heads.

First, Garcia laid hands on the head of the lady who couldn't feed herself and couldn't even talk and prayed for her. Immediately, her head quit shaking. She looked up at Brother David and said, "Are you Jesus?"

Brother Garcia laughed and said, "No, Jesus is in me, and I prayed for you in the Name of Jesus, but I'm not Jesus. But Jesus just healed you!"

She looked at him for a long time and finally said, "Can I get up?"

Garcia smiled and said, "Yes, I told you in the name Jesus, get up and walk!"

The once-crippled lady got up and started walking and then started doing a waltz type dance—a beautiful dance as if she were a young woman. She danced for at least an hour.

Brother Garcia smiled at her beautiful dancing then looked around at the other woman. With a big smile on her face, she simply said, "I'm ready."

He came over and prayed for her, and in a minute she was up. She kind of stood there shaking—as if she were afraid. Brother David reached out to steady her, but she said, "No, leave me alone; pray for him." Sister Carney had already gotten the footrests up on all the wheelchairs and had moved on to someone else.

Brother Garcia prayed for the man and the crippled man asked, "What is this? It's like electricity."

Garcia simply replied, "It's the Power of God. You're healed in the Name of Jesus, and you can get up and walk or run or dance or whatever you want to do."

I asked, "Well, what did he do?"

Garcia replied, "He took off in a streak running as I just stood there marveling at all three of them celebrating their healings."

Brother David then would tell me his most endearing miracle. A little Hispanic girl, about the age of six, was blind. Her eyes were gray—a scary looking gray. Her parents told him that she started going blind at about the age of two and was completely blind by the time she was four. He prayed for the child, and when she opened her eyes, the gray was gone, replaced with beautiful black eyes. She had been instantly healed. The child started dancing and celebrating, screaming the Name of Jesus while her parents tried to keep up with her.

Brother Garcia also recalled a man in his mid-thirties, who had a gum disease. His face was almost a dark red due to poison in his gums, which were a blackish color because of his teeth rotting. He laid hands on the man and prayed, and then told him to open his mouth. He asked the man if he felt anything and the man replied, "Yeah. I feel something."

Brother Garcia said, "I don't think so. You didn't feel anything because nothing happened here. Close your mouth again." Garcia prayed a second time and asked, "Feeling anything?"

"A little."

Garcia replied, "We're not getting it done." Before he prayed a third time, he asked, "Do you believe God is going to give you new gums, new teeth, and He's going to clear up this infection in your face? Do you understand that is what we're praying for? You're going to get healed,"

In obedience, the man said, "Okay."

Garcia prayed and this time the redness disappeared from the man's face. When the man opened his mouth, his gums were turning pink, and to Garcia's astonishment, he saw rotten teeth heal. By the time the man left the meeting that evening, he was completely healed!

I had the privilege of meeting the man's son, Bill, at Pisgah when Brother Smith introduced him to me. I had several conversations with Bill and finally asked the question I was dying to ask. "Bill," I said, "Did your dad have bad teeth when he died?" Bill just grinned at the question and told me that in fact, at the time of his death, his dad had a full set of perfect teeth in his head.

Brother Garcia summed up his experience with God at Azusa with these words: "When you came into Azusa, you got healed. The more you attended, the more faith you had, and the more things would happen. Because your faith was building up as you saw other people believing and you believed, soon you had no doubt when you walked up to someone that they were going to get healed. After a while it was easy to have the boldness to walk up to someone and proclaim "God is going to heal you tonight!"

I understood why Brother Garcia desired to once again be a part of the Shekinah Glory and see the miraculous hand of God move among His people. It was forty years ago that we spoke, and Brother Garcia told of the 100 year prophesy by Brother Seymour concerning the fresh outpouring of God's Spirit. As this book is being written, people all over the world are celebrating the Azusa Centennial.

I pray the prayer of my dear friend and brother, David Garcia, that soon we will see Brother Seymour's prophesy fulfilled and the greatest visitation of God ever known to man fall fresh on this world.

*Charles Parham also prophesied that another great revival would happen in about 100 years. Seymour, who made the prophecy around 1909 or 1910 may have made this prophesy after Parham.

SUFFER THE LITTLE CHILDREN

Meet Sister Dundee

Azusa Age: 22

Every miracle at Azusa Street was a time for rejoicing. Twenty-four hours a day the Warehouse was full of people celebrating over the mighty movement of God as the blind were given sight, the crippled were able to walk, the sick were made well, and the diseased were made whole. The thought that God visited us in a barn to introduce His Son and revisited us through the Shekinah Glory in a warehouse that was once a stable confounds the minds of scholars and skeptics. These miracles were happening in an old, run-down church that had been abandoned and once used to house animals. By the time the building was rented for the revival meetings, it wasn't even fit for animals.

We keep building great temples and cathedrals with lavish decorations and furnishings, and He keeps showing up in the most humble of dwellings. Perhaps there is a lesson here as we watch for the outpouring of His Spirit and the return of His Shekinah Glory to fall upon us once again.

For over three years at Azusa, there was much to rejoice about but nothing more precious than the healing of His little children. What gives us more joy and grateful hearts than to see a little child restored? A dear Saint of Azusa, whom I had the honor to know, understood and experienced such joy over and over again as she was led to seek out the little children and assist in bringing healing to their sick or broken bodies.

Sister Dundee had been around Pisgah since the years of Dr. Yoakum. She even had a grandson, Teddy, who lived with Brother Smith and his family. While I was at Pisgah, she remarried. I often thought about her new husband's devotion to Sister Dundee and how they were such a beautiful, sweet couple. I also was kind of partial to him because he would take Teddy and me to eat breakfast at a lot of the better restaurants. Sister Dundee was close to 80 years old when I met her. Her hair, black with a bit of gray, was pulled back into a glory bun. Italian by birth, Sister Dundee was a very quiet, sweet woman. She wore gold-rimmed glasses that hung or slid down to the end of her nose. Like Sister Carney, she wore those small granny boots with the hooks and eyelets. She was very healthy for her age and very well spoken.

She had experienced all kinds of miracles at Azusa, but I would have to coax and pull the stories out of her. When she was at Azusa, she liked being around Sister Carney and adored Brother Anderson— relationships that continued at Pisgah. When I went to her home to hear her stories, her husband would sit on the floor right next to me, his face beaming. He was just as excited as I was because he couldn't get her to tell *him* those stories when they were by themselves.

Sister Dundee began her stories by telling about the crippled child on crutches, about seven or eight years old, brought to the meeting by her mother. The child had normal-sized legs but wore braces and needed crutches to walk. The child told Sister Dundee that she had been prayed for before, but nothing had happened to her. Sister Dundee sat down and talked to her and explained that if she got healed, it would bring great glory to Jesus. She told the child, "You are supposed to get healed at Azusa."

The little girl listened to her and said, "Okay. Pray for me."

Sister Dundee asked, "Has anyone ever taken your braces off before they prayed for you?"

"No."

Sister Dundee said, "Well, that needs to stop."

Together, they took the braces off the little girl while she was sitting down, and then Sister Dundee took the braces and crutches over to the other side of the room and came back to her. She gently smiled at her and said, "Now, you can't get those back because I won't bring them back to you, and I will keep your mother busy so she can't get them for you. You're just going to have to get healed. Darling, we've got to glorify Jesus. It would break His heart if you didn't get healed."

Tears welled up in the little girl's eyes as she almost started to cry. Sister Dundee told her, "All that is left for us to do is to start praying and obey Jesus and you will be healed. Then Jesus will get the glory."

The little girl agreed, and Sister Dundee prayed for her. Within a few moments, the little girl said that she felt something in her feet—something she had never felt before! Sister Dundee told her to stand up and to start trying to move her feet. The little girl said, "I can't!"

Sister Dundee gently responded, "You need to try."

You could see the excitement rise as the little girl started moving her feet up and down. She looked down and started doing a dance like a little stomp. Then she started screaming that she was healed. Sister Dundee turned her loose, and she went dancing and stomping all over the warehouse. *This time*, the little girl was healed.

Sister Dundee loved picking out children and ministering to them—the younger the child, the better she liked it. Her next story was the most tender of all the Azusa stories. She went to a child not yet a year old with a bow in the neck. The baby would not cry or make any noise, but the mother said that she could tell that the baby was in pain. Sister Dundee asked the mother if she could pray for her baby. When the mother agreed, she took the child from her, putting the baby blanket over its head so that the mother couldn't see.

She prayed for the baby, and tried not to get too excited because she was holding the baby in her arms. She had to contain herself when the bow started to disappear. She told me that she had to make sure not to throw a "Pentecostal fit."

When the bow straightened out, Sister Dundee just stood there crying as the baby looked up at her and smiled. Finally, she heard the mother ask what was happening. "Why are you crying? Is there something wrong with my baby?"

Sister Dundee was standing there loving on the child as she pulled the blanket back and showed the smiling, healed baby to her.

I asked, "Did you give the baby back to its mother?"

Sister Dundee said, "Oh, Lord, no, I couldn't have caught that mother if I had wanted to. The mother just went running around rejoicing!"

I asked about the father, and she said that the father wasn't at the meeting, but Sister Dundee had met him later. The mother took the baby back home and showed the father his healed baby. Not only did he come to the revival after that, he got saved and became the pastor of one of the larger churches in the Los Angeles area for about 35-plus years.

Sister Dundee also told of a little boy that had to have his head and his body strapped into his wheelchair to hold him up. She went over to the boy, and asked his parents, "What is wrong with him?"

The parents were not exactly sure. He had some kind of paralysis but could breathe on his own. She told them, "Well, this is good, for the Lord's Name will be glorified, but we can't just pray for him and leave him tied up here." Sister Dundee started undoing the strap on his neck and told his parents to hold his body up. After she got everything loosened, she laid her hands on him and cried out, "In the Name of Jesus Christ, be made perfectly whole." Sister Dundee said that immediately the boy jerked and then wanted to get down to play.

I asked, "Well, how old was he?"

Sister Dundee said, "Maybe he was six."

I said, "You mean a little bitty kid?"

Sister Dundee just smiled and said, "Yes, a little bitty kid. I no longer had gotten the words 'In the Name of Jesus' out, and he was healed."

Sister Dundee told me that she got to see this boy many times over the next three years during the revival and about a year after that. The little boy affectionately call Sister Dundee "Mammy" from the time of his healing up until the last time she saw him.

There were other miracles Sister Dundee participated in—some of them with adults. She too loved the Shekinah Glory and loved the music that fell on the people as they sang in the Spirit. She described the music as like a choir from heaven coming down to join in the singing. She was part of Azusa almost the entire time the revival lasted. She loved it all, but nothing compared to the love she felt for the children in need of a miracle. Throughout her life, including while she was at Pisgah, God used her to touch the lives of children with miracles and healings.

PREPARING FOR THE MIRACULOUS

Meet Brother Fox

Azusa Age: 18

Azusa had global ramifications. Not only did people come to Azusa from all over the world, many went back home to their native countries, healed, renewed, inspired, transformed, and ready to be used of God. Azusa was a *hands-on workshop for the miraculous* led by God Himself. God used this great outpouring not only to meet immediate needs but also for preparation to serve Him throughout the world. He brought young people there to train them for the mission field both at home and across the world. Men and women alike discovered the awesome power of God and how to be used of Him to perform His mighty works.

One such man was Brother Fox. When he was in his late teenage years, he went to Azusa in preparation to go to the mission field, or in particular to India and labor for God. By the time he arrived at Azusa, Ralph Riggs was about fourteen and C.W. Ward was around sixteen. For about 18 months, Brother Fox experienced and participated in the miracles and healings at the Warehouse. By the time he reached his twentieth birthday, he was using what he had learned at Azusa to bring the mighty life-changing power of God to India.

When I met Brother Fox in 1963, he had just retired and settled at Pisgah where he renewed his friendships with many Azusa Saints. He was in his early seventies, stood around five feet, nine inches tall, and weighed about 150 pounds. He kept his shiny silver hair kind of long and combed straight back. His hair was so shiny that when he got around a light, it would glow. I had the privilege of riding with him on a trolley from time to time when he would go and witness to those riding the cable cars, and in between his witnessing, as we traveled, I would listen to his stories about India. But, when it came to stories about Azusa, I went to his apartment, settled at his feet with my cookies and milk, and listened intently.

He shared with me that he was awestruck by the movement of God and how the manifestation of God's power varied according to the degree of the manifestation of the Shekinah Glory—the thicker the cloud, the greater the miracles. He was also in awe of Brother Seymour. Fox said that this man had to be a very deep man of God.

Fox was present at the miracle when the man's arm grew out of the socket. During that experience, Brother Fox heard from God that he himself would have miracles like Seymour's, but in a foreign country—a word that proved itself over and over again as Brother Fox labored in India. Fox took the anointing with him when he left Azusa, but he could not take with him the

Shekinah Glory. He explained to me that as far as he could tell, the Shekinah Glory was unique to the Azusa Street Revival.

While at Azusa, Brother Fox went around being used by God to heal everybody he could. He loved to pray for the deaf and the mute. He would pray for them and whisper in each ear, "You deaf spirit, you come out in the Name of Jesus." He said he could hear a little pop and "whishing" sound as the ear would be healed, then he would go to the next person and do the same.

If they couldn't talk, he laid hands on their necks. He said, "I'm not one of those who would stick my hand down their mouths—they might get excited and bite a finger off." He told me that he prayed in the Name of Jesus and sometimes they would start talking. Most of the time though they would have to learn how to talk but they would start making audible sounds.

Brother Fox remembered a man with his neck blackened by a cancer that had eaten up his throat leaving him unable to talk. Fox prayed for him, laying hands on the lump that protruded from his neck. Looking down at the blackened area after the prayer, Brother Fox said, "I don't see anything happening; something is wrong here." He asked the man, "Are you believing?"

The man nodded his head.

"Let's do it again." With those words, Brother Fox prayed again. This time when he took his hands away, the blackness and lump were gone. He commanded the man, "Talk!"

The man blurted out, "I can't!"

Fox said, "Say that again."

The man realized that a miracle had taken place, and he could talk. The cancer was gone, and his throat was restored. Immediately, the man started rejoicing and shouting. Brother Fox just stood there being the reserved gentleman that he was, but you could see the smile as he stood in awe of the miracle.

God was preparing Brother Fox for great and mighty works in India. One lesson he was taught by the Spirit was that you didn't have to heal people one at a time. He recalled when a sign-language teacher brought his class of totally deaf people from a school for the deaf to the meeting.

"If you want to teach them to sign why did you bring them to a place where they would get healed? You're going to be out of a job because these people are going to be healed tonight." Brother Fox took the teacher by surprise.

The teacher responded with apparent disbelief, "You're talking like they are *all* going to get healed."

"They are! They all are going to be healed!" Brother Fox spoke, emboldened by God's Spirit.

This was a group of around 35 deaf people. Without wavering, Brother Fox gestured and told them all to join hands and form a circle. He looked at the teacher, standing nearby, and told the teacher, "Evidently, you don't have much faith, so stand off to the side."

"Now, I'm going to lay hands on this man and start with him." Immediately, Fox realized that they couldn't understand a word he was saying, and the teacher was laughing at him because he too understood that they couldn't hear him. Without hesitation, Brother Fox simply whispered in the first man's ear and told the spirit to come out. The miracle was immediate. As soon as the once-deaf man could hear, he got excited and when the others saw his excitement and that he could hear, they started getting healed one by one like a line of dominoes— in just a few minutes *all* of them were healed. Fox had only touched the first man in the circle. From that point on, God took over and allowed His power to flow through the connected hands touching each and everyone gathered in the circle.

I sat and listened to Brother Fox tell his stories both about Azusa and India and the mighty miracles God used him to perform. I couldn't help but remember the words recorded in the Gospel of John.* Jesus told His disciples, "He that believeth on Me, the works that I do shall he also do; and greater works than these shall he do..."

Brother Fox had a strong and mighty belief in the power of Jesus. He went to God's workshop and saw with his very eyes the wonder-working power of God. He was used of God at Azusa to perform mighty works and took the lessons he had learned at Azusa and applied them to his work in India. There the blind found sight, the lame could walk, the sick found health, and mighty healings were commonplace. The Spirit of God worked mightily through Brother Fox. The only thing he didn't have was the Shekinah Glory.

*John 14:12

FOUND FAITHFUL

Meet Sister Goldie
Azusa Age: 18

"Moreover is it required in stewards, that a man be found faithful."* Paul's words are timeless but never more appropriate than for those touched by God at Azusa. The parable of talents found in Matthew 25, stresses that God gives us abilities according to His divine purpose, and we are to be faithful with what we have been given. With God, it is not the number of abilities that is important; it is the use of our God-given abilities that God rewards.

The abilities of those used by God at Azusa were diverse. God was preparing some for great and mighty tasks and others simply to be found faithful day-by-day using their God-given abilities for His Glory.

Sister Goldie is one of the Azusa Saints who is worthy of the commendation that she was faithful in her service to God. You may remember her when we first started this book, for she was the one used of God to lead me to know Jesus Christ as my personal Savior. She was also the one who introduced me to many of the Azusa Saints residing at Pisgah. In the initial chapters, I told you about her ministry at Venice Beach and Pisgah. In this chapter, I want to share her stories about her days at Azusa.

Sister Goldie came from Venice Beach to Pisgah once a month. She always arrived early so she could tell me her stories. Faithful to the tradition that was common among the Saints, she brought with her homemade chocolate chip cookies and cold milk that she had purchased from Dick's Market after she got off the bus. With cookies and cold milk in hand, she would walk down to Pisgah.

The truth is, she spoiled me rotten. She bought me my first Bible, engraved with my name on it. She bought me my first dress coat and dress shoes. I was her "little" project, and she loved ministering to me. I was like a son to her; in fact, at times she even referred to me as her son.

We would meet in the back of the dining hall where there were couches and chairs. At first, it was just us, but after a few months, she began to draw an audience of young people and adults who just wanted to hear her stories about the mighty works of God. She needed very little coaxing. One of the main reasons she came to Pisgah each month was to tell her stories, and she loved the opportunity to relive those moments she spent serving God at Azusa.

When she was about 18 years old, she started attending the Azusa revival in 1908, and attended for about two years. She was already a Christian and didn't need healing, but she wanted to be a part of what was happening at Azusa Street.

She got involved with Sister Carney and asked her how she did what she did. Sister Carney explained that they were part of a great revival that she and others had prayed for God to send. Sister Carney further explained that they worked with the people gathered for the meeting until Brother Seymour came down. They continued to minister to the people even while Brother Seymour had the box on his head. She told Sister Goldie, "Even after he comes down, we have between ten minutes to an hour while Brother Seymour has the box on his head. When he takes the box off, you go sit down." Goldie watched Carney for a few days—what she did and how she did it—then started finding people to bless.

Sister Goldie was drawn to people with obvious disfigurements. One such young man had a bow in his arm. He had broken his arm in a ballgame at school several years prior. For some reason, he never saw a doctor, and the bones had never been reset. She looked at the man and said, "This is going to be fun."

The young man looked at her and said, "It's going to be what?"

Sister Goldie repeated herself, "It's going to be fun." She took his deformed arm in one hand and touched the bowed bones with her other hand. She looked straight at the arm and said, "I take all authority over you and I command you in the Name of Jesus, straighten out!" Immediately and miraculously, the arm healed and straightened—no noise, no popping—and quietly became normal.

She was drawn to people who had disfigurements or ugly growths on their faces and would pray for them. After the first couple of healings where the growths or tumors just fell off in her hand, she began to carry towels with her. Sometimes she had to bandage the area where the growth had been because the tumors or growths would come off and leave a wound in the flesh. Sometimes, the total miracle was not instantaneous. The tumor would come off, but the complete healing may have taken hours—even overnight. As she prayed for these people, the growth, goiter, tumor or whatever would come off in Sister Goldie's hand.

She would seek people out. Most people just tolerated small growths on their faces and didn't seek healing, but Sister Goldie had other thoughts. She was instrumental in healing perhaps 3,000 tumors and facial growths during the two years she attended the revival services.

From Azusa to Venice Beach, from 1908 until her death, this dear Saint was found faithfully serving God with each and every gift and ability He had entrusted to her. She has since gone on to be with the Lord, and I am certain she heard the words, "Well done My good and faithful servant."

*1 Corinthians 4:2

LIFE BEYOND AZUSA
Meet Brother Brown
Azusa Age: 16

"I shall be telling this with a sigh someday ages and ages hence. Two roads diverged in a yellow wood..." So wrote Robert Frost in his famous poem, "The Road Not Taken". Throughout this book, we have shared the stories of Azusa Saints ages and ages hence—some 60 years later. The Azusa Street Revival ended in 1910. For a host of possible reasons, the Shekinah Glory left—never to return. The effects of Azusa on the lives of those who were there were as varied as the people themselves.

At least two great denominations, The Assemblies of God and The Church of God in Christ, were born out of Azusa by leaders such as Ralph Riggs, C.W. Ward, and Charles Harrison Mason. We met two men, Brother Fox and Brother Lake, who went on to serve the Lord in a powerful way as missionaries to India and South Africa. Two of these dear Saints went on to establish missions for the downtrodden and needy. One man traveled throughout the Midwestern United States leading revivals and founding churches. There is no question that for many, life beyond Azusa was but a continuation of serving God.

There were others who just allowed Azusa to be a footnote in their lives. Once the miracles ceased, and life got back to the normal and ordinary, Azusa just lived in faded memories. Then there were others so impressed with Azusa that life just stopped there. Like Peter on the Mount of Transfiguration*, who wanted to build three tabernacles and just stay there with Jesus forever, there were some Saints who spent the remainder of their lives just reliving the memories and basking in the glory of days past when Azusa was alive and well.

I met such a man in 1960. Bill Brown had arrived and retired at Pisgah just about six months before my arrival. When I met him, he stood several inches over six feet, and had a medium build, weighing around 200 pounds. He lived in the dormitory with me and constantly wanted to talk about Azusa—in fact that is all he wanted to talk about. From time to time, we would go down to the dining hall, and he would be in "heaven" as he got a chance to relive his days at Azusa.

At Azusa, Brother Brown loved ministering to those who were blind. He shared with me that while there, he was involved in participating in the healing of over 50 blind people, and each and every time the healing was instantaneous.

I asked Brother Brown if any particular healing stood out in his mind, and he shared the story of a woman whose eyes were totally dark, almost black, with no white showing anywhere. The whites of her eyes had never developed, and she had been blind from birth. The reason

124

this miracle stood out in his memory is that when she opened her eyes after he prayed for her, and she realized she could see, the lady let out a loud, blood-curdling scream that caused him to jump back in momentary fear. When her eyes opened and Brother Brown saw the whites of her eyes, he was just about ready to start shouting himself, but her scream was so sudden and unexpected it caught him by surprise. After the shock wore off, they both began to rejoice.

All of his miracles were not with the blind. He participated in miracles for the crippled, deformed, and those confined to wheelchairs due to illness or physical disabilities. He recalled one time going up to a man who was lying on a cot. Brother Brown asked him, "Do you want to be healed? Do you want to take up your cot and carry it home?"

The man looked up and smiled. "Yes." His response was simple, but clear. Brother Bill prayed for him, and immediately, he got up, folded up his cot, then went around worshipping God. Before the man left the meeting, he went back to where he had been confined to the cot, picked it up, and carried his cot away while rejoicing that he had been healed.

While Sister Carney and Brothers Ward, Riggs, and Anderson were running around seeking out people to minister to, Brother Brown was more subdued. Being more of a loner, he wandered around looking for blind people to whom he could minister.

That was then. Even after the departure of the Shekinah Glory, for the next several years, Brother Brown would return to the Azusa Street Church where Seymour still preached. He didn't go there with anticipation of seeing God move mightily, rather he went back there moping around, saddened by the loss of what had been. He would sit in the service and weep for the loss of yesterday.

In 1960, there were no blind people being healed by Brother Brown. There was no legacy of being used by God as a minister or missionary. In fact, he had nothing but regrets. He told me that he had spent a lifetime remembering Azusa, but never moved on. He would wistfully tell me that he should have been preaching the Gospel, or that he should have been a missionary like Brother Fox, but regretfully, he told me, he had missed God's purpose or will for his life. For over fifty years, he lived in the past, sitting around daydreaming about the yesteryears of Azusa. Wasted years!

Now retired with his productive years behind him, he settled among the Saints of Azusa where he could share his stories with those who would understand and welcome his additions to the Azusa legacy. But when he wasn't sharing his past, he was sad, if not miserable. Somehow, yesterday doesn't fulfill today's cravings to experience God in a fresh and vital way.

Often, I would leave my meeting with Brother Brown with mixed emotions. I shared his joy of Azusa, but I felt helpless when faced with the sadness of this dear brother. How could one who had been used of God to heal so many who were blind, have been so blind?

*Matthew 17:4

MAY WE SEEK AND EXPERIENCE GOD DAILY

My prayer for all of us is, "Dear Lord, don't let me miss You! Use me everyday in a mighty way. Let me feel Your Presence and Your fresh renewal each and every day of my life. I thank You for the memories of yesterday, but I need to experience You today and expect great things from You tomorrow. Yesterday is gone, but today and tomorrow I live in expectation of a new and wonderful outpouring of Your Mighty Spirit all around me. Amen!"

Azusa Youth Tell Their Stories

Discover the Azusa Code

Prophecies made during the Azusa Visitation of God at the beginning of the twentieth century tell us that 100 years after Azusa, God will once again visit us sometime between 2009-2010, depending on exactly when this prophesy was made. Although we don't know the exact date, God does, and He will be on time. From all that we can discern, the year of 2008 is the year of preparation! We who hunger for His return and the return of the Shekinah Glory must prepare the way.

What are we to be doing? The Azusa outpouring gives us the blueprint for preparing for His Visitation just prior to the Second Coming of His dear Son.

The Uniqueness of Azusa

The dawning of the twentieth century ushered in an event that was so powerful that it changed the course of Christianity. In 1906, God actually, physically, took up residence at 312 Azusa Street in Los Angeles, California. This was the first time since the Wilderness Wanderings of the Israelites that God had a physical address here on earth. Then His address was the Tabernacle in care of Moses, in 1906-1910 His address was Azusa Street!

Since the earthly ministry of Jesus Christ and Pentecost, the most significant, most influential, life-transforming event in the life of Christianity was The Azusa Visitation beginning in 1906. Approximately 2000 years prior, Jesus was born, cradled in a lowly stable and publicly God dwelt among us in the form of His Son for about three and one-half years. In 1906, God chose to visit us publicly and chose a stable—an old Methodist church that had been converted to a stable—to cradle His visitation for about three and one-half years.

Azusa was a planned, well-orchestrated work of God brought to fulfillment when all the pieces were in place, and at least a small group of people were prepared to host His visitation. God reintroduced His mighty power—power that is available to anyone willing to surrender to the Spirit that dwells within. For over three years, God performed miracle after miracle and healing after healing as people entered into His holy presence. Heaven truly came down and thousands who came into His presence experienced His glory.

THE AZUSA CODE

There is much about Azusa that will remain a mystery, but there is much we do know—especially about what was going on in Los Angeles that both prepared the way and created the spiritual environment where God could dwell for over three years. There is much about

Azusa that suggests that there were certain behaviors, disciples, and desires that were significant.

As we study the stories, we discover a code. A code is simply a systematic collection of rules of procedures or conduct. Azusa is more than an historical event to be celebrated every 100 years. Azusa was God's blueprint for constructing the elements necessary before His visitation and dwelling among His creation. Within the experiences of Azusa is a collection of procedures or conduct that was critical to the event of Azusa. In fact, the Azusa Code resembles a "code" given to the Children of Israel in II Chronicles 7:14. Read the words that God spoke to Solomon after the building of the temple:

"If my people, which are called by my name shall *humble [humility]* themselves and *pray [prayer]*, and *seek my face [obedience]*, and *turn from their wicked ways [purity]*; *then will I hear from heaven [exectation]*, and will forgive their sin, and will heal their land." (Italics added)

This is a code. Note that there are a collection of procedures or conduct that when practiced will bring about desired results.

Not only was there a specific Azusa Code, it is the exact code spoken in II Chronicles 7:14. Those involved in the Azusa Experience did not copy this code from II Chronicles. Nobody was preaching this code for people to follow. In fact the code only becomes noticeable by overlaying the Azusa Experience over the code given to Solomon.

Heaven Came Down

Miracles and healings abounded at Azusa, but if you focus on the miracles and healings you will miss the most important aspect of Azusa. Miracles and healings were the signs of a far greater wonder that was taking place at Azusa. Spiritual gifts were in abundance during the days of Azusa, but if you focus on the gifts you miss the greatest gift ever bestowed on man since the incarnation and sacrificial life and death of Christ.

Azusa was a time when the Shekinah Glory came down and manifested itself for over three years at 312 Azusa Street. Shekinah Glory is the physical manifestation of the elements that form the sanctuary that houses the very presence of God. This was the uniqueness of Azusa. This is what makes Azusa different from other great revivals and movements.

Using the foolish and common to confound the skeptics and the scoffers, God Himself intersected history once again in a most unexpected manner. God pitched his tent and dwelt among us. Allow me to introduce you to the AZUSA CODE

GOD'S FORMULA HASN'T CHANGED

H.O.P₂.E. For the Outpouring of God's Presence

Azusa has often been imitated but never duplicated. God has a formula and a timetable that is His and His alone.

In about 1910, William Seymour prophesied that God would visit His people in about a hundred years. Now that the hundred years are upon us, there is anticipation that we will soon experience the Shekinah Glory like the Azusa Saints at the turn of the twentieth century. This will only happen if God's people follow God's formula. Thousands of years ago, God told His people that if they would humble themselves and pray and seek His face and turn from their wicked ways, then He would hear their prayers and forgive their sins and heal their land (2Chr 7:14).

Azusa showed us this formula in action. This great outpouring can be summarized by five basic characteristics: Humility, Obedience, Prayer and Purity, and Expectation—the foundation of 2 Chronicles 7:14. These five requirements spell out the acrostic H.O.P₂.E., and indeed within these requirements is our HOPE for God's outpouring of His Presence on His people.

Humility is God's style. Remember the stable that was used at Bethlehem? Remember the stable that was used at Azusa? Remember the box over Brother Seymour's head?

Obedience was obvious. Those involved in ushering in this manifestation of God's Mighty Presence sought His face and truly turned from their wicked ways. There was a holiness at Azusa where people lived in strict obedience to God's commandment to love one another and to love God with all their heart.

Prayer was vital to God's visitation. Men and women had gathered months and years on their knees in fervent prayer, earnestly imploring God to send renewal and revival.

Purity is mandatory within the presence of God. Purity manifests love that is the environment in which God chooses to dwell.

Expectations were high. These men and women believed in their prayers. They were persistent and prayed in one accord, believing that God would hear the prayers of His Saints who in purity of heart and thought, totally surrendered to His Lordship. They prayed without ceasing and without doubt that soon they would experience the desires of their hearts.

Hope! Azusa is our anchor. We know God is listening and waiting to fall fresh on His people and His creation once again. He will come again and visit us before it is all over. We will see God in a Cloud of Glory—the Shekinah Glory—come and dwell among us. We will see His Mighty Spirit, clothed in fire, fall on us, exulting the Power of God. This is our HOPE, and steadfastly we hold to these beliefs.

DEAR LORD, USE US!

We know the time draws near for Your return. Someday soon, You will come in might and splendor. We know that someday soon every knee shall bow and confess You as King of Kings and Lord of Lords, triumphant in Your mission to bring redemption to creation.

We believe that soon, before Your final appearance as conquering King, we will again be honored by a great and might visitation and outpouring of Your Spirit. We believe that Azusa was but a foreshadowing of what will come just prior to the final days. As we seek to make ourselves worthy, hear the prayers of our hearts. Convict us of our sins as we seek Your face and turn from any wickedness that would separate us from You.

Isaiah captures our hearts. "We are all as an unclean thing, and all our righteousness is as filthy rags...but now, O Lord, thou art our father; we are the clay, and thou our potter; and we all are the work of thy hand."

Use us, as we humble ourselves, and fervently pray, and seek Your face and turn from our wicked ways, use us to usher in Your Visitation. Amen

DOES GOD WANT TO TOUCH YOUR LIFE?

• If you have been touched by these stories and want to make Jesus Christ your personal Savior, all God requires is:

1. **You Acknowledge you have sinned**
   We are told, "All have sinned and come short of the Glory of God" (Romans 3:23).

2. **You Believe and Confess that Jesus Christ is the Son of God who came to save you from your sin**
   Paul tells us, "If you will confess with your mouth the Lord Jesus, and believe in your heart that God raised Him from the dead, you will be saved" (Romans 10:9).

• If you desire to make Jesus your Lord and Savior, simply pray a prayer such as this:

"Dear Jesus, I confess I am a sinner in need of your saving grace. Forgive me of my sins, and come into my heart as my Lord and Savior. Thank you for hearing my prayer and giving me everlasting life."

If you just prayed that prayer, then welcome to the family of God! If you want to know more about your new life in Christ or more about the Baptism of the Holy Spirit and the Gifts these stories talk about, please contact us at Faith Family Church. You can contact Pastors Paul and Samantha Roach by calling: **1-800-611-4909.**

To Order Additional Books

You can order individual copies by
- Going to azusastories.com,
- Contacting Dare2dream Books at 405-642-8257,
- Or by contacting Billye Brim Ministries at 417-336-4877

Bookstores, Ministries, and Church Groups
can order in bulk:
20-99: $9 each s/h included
100+: $7.30 each s/h included
Call Dr. Jim Morris
405-642-8257
0r go to azusastories.com

To get in touch with Bro. Tommy call
405-410-9201

To get in touch with Dr. Morris
Email at dare2dreambooks@yahoo.com
Call: 405-642-8257

To get in touch with Cindy McCowan
Call 405-473-0704

137

Azusa Youth Tell Their Stories